BOTTOM OF THE

9 TH

GOD SPEAKS
TO ATHLETES
ABOUT THE
PAST,
PRESENT &
FUTURE

DR. ELLIOT JOHNSON

CROSS TRAINING
PUBLISHING

BOTTOM OF THE NINTH

Copyright © 1995 by Cross Training Publishing
P.O. Box 1541
Grand Island, NE 68802
308/384-5762

The print appearing on the cover of this book, 'Classic Chavez Clout' by William Purdom is published by Bill Goff Inc., P.O. Box 977, Kent, CT., 06757 (203) 927-1411. © William Purdom 1992

Library of Congress Cataloging-in-Publication Data

ISBN 1-887002-21-9
Johnson, Elliot
Elliot Johnson

BOTTOM OF THE NINTH / Elliot Johnson
Distributed in the United States and Canada by Cross Training Publishing

Cover illustrator: Jeff Sharpton
Printed in the United States of America

The Bottom of the 9th Inning
Introduction

IT'S BEEN A HARD-FOUGHT CONTEST. In the "Big Inning" (beginning) God created everything by His powerful word! Then man followed Satan in rebellion against the Creator and both sides became locked in fierce competition. In the home half of the seventh, Jesus Christ secured complete victory by His death, burial, and resurrection! The final outcome is certain! The Lord Jesus Christ defeated sin, death, and Satan! Because of His triumph, every person who trusts Him as Savior and Lord also wins!

We're now approaching the last inning — the bottom of the ninth — when Jesus will return to claim His draft choices (all true believers)!

As you study the entire "ballgame" from start to finish, may your expectation of His coming renew your excitement and commitment to our wonderful Savior and Lord!

Elliot Johnson

TABLE OF CONTENTS

First inning —
THE CREATION

The Real One . . .
JESUS CHRIST

Inning	1	2	3	4	5	6	7	8	9	10
SATAN	0									
GOD	Creation									

How They Scored

First inning —
The eternal God created the universe out of nothing . . .
He created man from dust . . . He Sovereignly adminis-
trates His creation from Heaven.

1

Read Genesis 1

In the beginning God created the heavens and the earth.

Genesis 1:1

First inning —
IN THE "BIG INNING" GOD . . .

A GOOD START is especially important if a baseball team is to make a strong run for the pennant. When a club gets too far behind, the psychological battle for even good teams is hard to win. A good start was even more important in 1994, as a strike disrupted the season and managers managed as though the season would be over in July . . . which it was!

God's account of His creation is brief and to the point. He does not intend to teach geology, physics or biology — though He knows everything there is to know about all three! If He had given the scientific details of creation, no one would understand it anyway! God wants us to know that He created the universe and He is the owner of it all. The idea of an evolutionary beginning without God is the invention of wicked minds to try to make themselves unaccountable to the God who created them and everything else. It has no scientific basis. Many of the leading scientists of the past (as well as those today) totally reject this idea. Biologist Edwin Conklin said, "The probability of life originating by accident is comparable to the probability of an unabridged dictionary originating from an explosion in a print shop." We know by faith that God made everything (Hebrews 11:1-3). The physical evidence confirms our faith in the powerful Creator.

Why did God create the heavens and the earth? Revelation 4:11 says, "You are worthy, our Lord and our God, to receive glory and honor and power, for you created all things, and by your will they were created and have their being." God created the universe because He wanted to create it. He created it for His glory and honor. God also created people for His glory (Isaiah 43:7). Are you glorifying God by the way you live?

3

Read Genesis 2

. . . the Lord God formed the man from the dust of the ground and breathed into his nostrils the breath of life, and the man became a living being.

Genesis 2:7

First inning —

THE LEAD-OFF MAN

IN BASEBALL a good lead-off man establishes the tempo of the offense. He is the first hitter the opposition faces, and he must consistently get on base. He must not strike out frequently. He should be fast enough to increase the odds of scoring via stolen bases, ground outs and base hits. In recent years, Ricky Henderson has become a prototypical lead-off man, for he possesses all these traits.

Adam was God's "lead-off" man for the human race. He was created from the earth and he was perfect. Adam was given everything necessary for happiness and fulfillment. He had plenty of good food. He was given work to develop his creativity. Adam's labor was service to God. It was his calling, his vocation. He was never bored in the Garden. He had authority over the animals and he named them all. He was given the woman (Eve) as a helper who was perfectly suitable to him. Finally, God gave man boundaries to provide security. But because God wanted man's voluntary worship, He gave man the freedom to choose to worship and serve his Creator. Man could accept God's plan and enjoy all His blessings, or he could rebel against God and suffer the consequences.

God made the ideal "lead-off" man. No form of evolution (theistic or otherwise) can account for human speech, human conscience, or the marvels of the human body. Only God knows how man best functions. He knows our needs, our joys, our sorrows, our weaknesses, and our strengths. He not only knows, He cares! Only a right relationship to God can keep us functioning as we were created to function.

4

Read Isaiah 46

Remember the former things, those of long ago; I am God, and there is no other; I am God and there is none like me. I make known the end from the beginning, from ancient times, what is still to come. I say: My prayer will stand, I will do all that I please.

Isaiah 46:9, 10

First inning —

SOVEREIGNTY OF THE UMPIRE

ONCE A BALLGAME STARTS the home-plate umpire has complete authority over the game. He makes calls as he sees them, though he is not always right because of his humanity. If rain falls, he decides when to call the grounds crew to put the tarp on the field. He decides when and if the game is postponed. As an impartial judge, the umpire is given the authority to rule the game.

If an umpire has authority over a ball game, God has even more supreme authority over His universe. *Nothing* happens that He does not either *cause* or *allow!* There is much that man does not *know*, did not *do*, and *can not do* concerning this universe (Job 38). We don't know how God created His universe. We can't create and we don't control His universe! It is *God's* universe! He is the Ruler of it all!

Many years after creation took place, man grew "too big for his britches." God sent prophets to remind men of His control! God said (through Isaiah) that it was His purpose that would stand. He will do all He pleases! He said, "Woe to him who quarrels with his Maker!" (Isaiah 45:9). "I am God, and there is no other; apart from me there is no God!" (Isaiah 45;5).

Jeremiah was another prophet who told of God's ultimate control. He wrote, "Oh, sovereign Lord, you have made the heavens and all earth by your great power and outstretched arm. Nothing is too hard for you" (Jeremiah 32:17). "Like clay in the hand of the potter, so are you in my hand, O house of Israel, said

5

the Lᴏʀᴅ" (Jeremiah 18:6). He went on to declare His sovereignty over nations and kingdoms!

The Lord said to Job, "Who has a claim against me that I must pay? Everything under heaven belongs to me!" (Job 41:11). Indeed, God answers to no one! After much suffering, Job replied, "I know that you can do all things; no plan of yours can be thwarted" (Job 42:2).

We must not criticize God for any reason. He is sovereignly in control of His world, including the circumstances of our lives. He knows what He is doing. We can trust Him to get us safely home!

Read Psalm 19

The heavens declare the glory of God; the skies proclaim the work of his hands.

Day after day they pour forth speech; night after night they display knowledge.

There is no speech or language where their voice is not heard.

Their voice goes out into all the earth, their words to all the ends of the world.

Psalm 19:1-4

First inning —
CREATOR AND SUSTAINER

MIKE MUSSINA, the Orioles' pitcher who has such an outstanding delivery, polished his motion as a child by imitating major league pitchers he had seen on television. It takes constant work to sustain good habits, but the result is pinpoint control of all his pitches. Mussina's control didn't just happen by chance. It required much care and supervision.

Our material universe didn't just happen. It isn't sustained by chance either. The 93 million miles from earth to sun is just right to sustain life. The 23 1/2 degree tilt of the earth ensures seasonal changes and a minimum of desert. The ozone layer protects us from deadly ultraviolet rays from the sun. The oxygen (21%)/ nitrogen (78%) mixture is perfect for breathing. Nothing was left to chance by our wise Creator.

The Psalms, Proverbs, and Ecclesiastes are books of poetry that are filled with wisdom. They tell us of the creating and sustaining power of Almighty God. Psalm 19 says that day in and day out the heavens "pour forth speech" declaring God's glory. Ecclesiastes 3:14 says that everything God does endures forever. It is God who both creates and sustains His universe by His natural laws, precepts and commands. He sends lightning, thunder, and rain (Psalm 77:17, 18). Psalm 148:8 tells

7

us the lightning, hail, snow, and clouds, and stormy winds all do His bidding! He established day and night, sun and moon, and summer and winter (Psalm 74:16, 17). Abundant showers come from our God (Psalm 68:7-9). The wind is His messenger and fire His servant (Psalm 104:5).

He makes grass grow for the cattle and plants for man to cultivate — bringing forth food from the earth (Psalm 104:14). All animals look to Him to feed them at the proper time (v. 27). Our God is consistently powerful in His sustaining provision for the earth.

The New Testament sheds further light upon His mighty power in His universe. John 1:1 tells us that Jesus Christ, the living Word of God created everything. Colossians 1:15-17 reveals even more of the grandeur of Jesus:

> "He is the image of the invisible God, the firstborn over all creation. For by him all things were created: things in heaven and on earth, visible and invisible, whether thrones or powers or rulers or authorities; all things were created by him and for him. He is before all things, and in him all things hold together."

Science can't tell us why the very core of the atom stays together. Since like charges repel, the protons at the core should fly apart causing *everything* to disintegrate! The Bible tells us the answer! Jesus Christ holds all things together! If He were to withdraw His hand for one second, creation would disintegrate into oblivion! Praise the name of our great Creator and Sustainer!

Second inning —

THE FALL
AND THE PROMISE

The Real One . . .
JESUS CHRIST

Inning	1	2	3	4	5	6	7	8	9	10
SATAN	0	Fall								
GOD	Creation	Promise								

How They Scored

Second inning —
Satan tempts man to disobey God and serve him . . .
Man falls and is separated from God . . . banned from
Eden . . . sin pays off with death . . . creation subjected
to frustration . . . God promises to redeem both man
and creation.

9

Read Genesis 3:1-7

When the woman saw that the fruit of the tree was good for food and pleasing to the eye, and also desirable for gaining wisdom, she took some and ate it. She also gave some to her husband, who was with her, and he ate it.

Genesis 3:6

Second inning —
THE GREAT KNOCKDOWN PITCH

RECENTLY, PROFESSIONAL PITCHERS have intentionally thrown at hitters with alarming frequency. Though the tactic has been in use for decades, it seems to have become more in vogue in the 90s. It is used to intimidate the hitter and his team. Many times a hitter will charge the mound starting a full-scale team brawl. Such events are very harmful to both players and the game of baseball.

Satan threw a fatal "knockdown pitch" at mankind in the Garden of Eden. The ensuing brawl between man and Satan, man and God, and man and his fellow man has scarred the entire race. Disguised as a beautiful snake (which probably walked upright), Satan approached the woman and tricked her with his crafty, sly questioning of God's instructions and deceived Eve (2 Corinthians 11:3), appealing to a desire to be "like God." He masqueraded as an "angel of light" (2 Corinthians 11:14, 15), as do the New Age proponents who teach we can become gods. Eve saw the fruit, desired it, took it, ate it, and gave some to Adam, who ate, sinning with the full knowledge that he was disobeying God (1 Timothy 2:13, 14). This was one time when a man should not have listened to his wife!

Sin never involves only the sinner. It is never only private. Eve's sin included Adam, who then involved the entire human race (Romans 5:12). Physical and spiritual death (separation from God) has been passed on to all men because we have inherited the sin nature from our

11

first parents. It wasn't that the fruit of the tree of the knowledge of good and evil was evil in and of itself. In fact, man did gain a knowledge only God possessed (Genesis 3:22). Man learned about the presence of evil, but he gained this knowledge independent of God. *That* was his sin. God did not want man *to experience* evil. But, sad to say, man disobeyed God and now saw good and evil from the perspective of evil. He became a sinner!

Satan's "knockdown pitch" has resulted in brutal, global brawls since that day. The sin of man always has paid off in death. Satan's lies never come true. It is the fear of the Lord, not Satan's lies (Proverbs 1:7) that is the beginning of wisdom. Only God could rescue man from the terrible fall he had now experienced.

Read Genesis 3:7-24

So the Lord God banished him from the Garden of Eden to work the ground from which he had been taken.

Genesis 3:23

Second inning —
THROWN OUT OF THE GAME

ON SEPTEMBER 25, 1993, the Colorado Buffaloes took on the powerful Miami Hurricanes in a matching of highly-ranked football powers. But as thrilling as the 35-29 Miami victory was, it was overshadowed by a bench-clearing brawl that delayed the game almost 20 minutes. Officials were unable to control the melee, so they stepped back and wrote down the numbers of the various offenders. When the punching, gouging, and kicking was over, the referees ejected seven Miami players and five from Colorado. What began as a day of excitement ended in banishment and disappointment for 12 athletes.

Banishment and sorrow also resulted for Adam, Eve, and all mankind because of the sin of rebellion in the Garden of Eden. When Adam sinned, he discovered evil by experience. He knew good, but became unable to do it. He knew evil and became unable to resist it! In his natural state, man became totally depraved. He became a coward and hid from God. He became ashamed of himself (the only correct emotion for those who have violated God's commands and forsaken His purposes). Then, he blamed Eve. Adam and Eve sewed fig leaves together to cover the organs that would reproduce them-selves and carry on the memory of their sin.

But God sought out man and provided a covering. Man's fig leaves (religion) are no substitute for the blood sacrifice God provides in restoring the relationship. An animal died to provide a covering. Adam and Eve prob-ably witnessed the death of the innocent animal to cover their guilt and sin. A curse was placed upon the ground and man was driven out of the Garden. God promised ultimate victory in the long struggle between good and evil (3:15). He did not want man to eat of the tree of life and live forever as sinners (3:22). Adam and Eve were "thrown out of the game." The only way man can eat of the tree of life (Revelation 22:2) is to be restored by faith in the sacrifice and covering God has provided in the death of the Lord Jesus Christ.

Read Romans 8:1-16

Therefore, there is now no condemnation for those who are in Christ Jesus.

Romans 8:1

Second inning —
PROMISE OF A RENEGOTIATED CONTRACT

IT WASN'T LONG AFTER Emmitt Smith's 1993 holdout and signing that Dallas' Troy Aikman wanted to renegotiated his own contract. Sure enough, Cowboy owner Jerry Jones soon tore up the old agreement and announced a new, renegotiated deal with his star quarterback. The agreement made Aikman the highest paid player in NFL history, calling for $50 million over eight years! All sides seemed happy as Dallas won the Super Bowl for the second consecutive year.

Immediately after man "broke his contract" with his loving heavenly Father, God announced a new "renegotiated contract!" Genesis 3:15 reveals that the offspring of Eve and the offspring of Satan would be in continual conflict. In other words, redeemed man would be in conflict with those who persisted in rebellion against God. There will be no peace until the final redemption of all things. It will be a long struggle. Genesis 3:15 initiates all prophecy, predicting that the seed of the woman (Jesus Christ) would crush Satan's head. He did so by dying on the cross for our sin, described as Satan "striking his heel." Though Adam and Eve couldn't understand it at the time, God had made His first promise, guaranteeing them a "new contract" with the Father!

It was God who sought out man to renegotiated this agreement. Man ran and hid himself, but God persisted in love to restore the fellowship with his erring creature. We did not first choose God, but He chose us (John 15:16). Romans 3:11 says that no one really seeks God.

15

It is He who first loved us (1 John 4:19). Salvation is entirely God's idea. If He hadn't sought us out in our lost condition, we would have been separated from Him forever!

What a wonderful plan He has devised! Our new contract is guaranteed! The blood of Christ promises all who are "in Christ" will never be condemned. Praise His Holy Name!

Read Romans 8:18-27

For the creation was subjected to frustration, not by its own choice, but by the will of the one who subjected it, in hope that the creation itself will be liberated from its bondage to decay and brought into the glorious freedom of the children of God.

Romans 8:20

Second inning —
CREATION FRUSTRATED

THE 1962 METS are known as probably the worst team in history. Marvelous Marv Throneberry characterized the team. On June 17, 1962, Marv hit what he thought was a clutch triple. As Met's fans cheered, the umpire called Throneberry out for missing first base. When manager Casey Stengel stormed out of the dugout in protest, his first base coach, Cookie LaVagetto, stopped him and said, "Don't bother, Case. He missed second base, too."

It is because of sin that man experiences frustration and futility. But that doesn't mean the '62 Mets were worse sinners! The Bible says that God's entire creation is subjected to frustration (futility, frailty, purposelessness) until the day when the curse is removed and creation is set free from bondage to decay. Tornadoes, hurricanes, floods, earthquakes, and drought are evidences of the imbalance brought on by the curse of sin. God not only cursed the serpent (crawl on its belly), the woman (pain in childbirth) and man (obstacles to making a living), but He also cursed the entire creation as part of His judgment on sin. The animals became ferocious and carnivorous. Extremes in temperature came about after the flood when God judged the world. If God did not keep His hand upon His creation, *everything* would be total frustration.

But God also planned for the salvation of mankind and the removal of the curse on creation. Some day, the physical world will be re-created! The creation "groans in agony, awaiting that glorious day of freedom!

17

As believers, we also "groan" inwardly as we await the removal of sin's curse and the final redemption of our bodies. We suffer in this life because of sin's curse. But we are winning! It may not seem like it when we are 0 for 4, a girlfriend or boyfriend leaves us, or we fail a test in school. Some have lost jobs, family, or their physical lives in representing Christ. But God is in the process of making us like Jesus (Romans 8:29) and *nothing* can stop Him!

This is not a runaway world over which God has lost interest or control. He is systematically guiding events to bring about His intended conclusion. We are winning the race, not through our own brilliance or strength, but through Christ. What a powerful Savior we have!

Third inning —
THE FLOOD

The Real One . . .
JESUS CHRIST

Inning	1	2	3	4	5	6	7	8	9	10
SATAN	0	Fall	0							
GOD	Creation	Promise	Flood							

How They Scored

Third inning —
Evil worsens . . . God warns man . . . Noah builds ark . . .
salvation offered to all, rejected by most . . . worldwide
flood . . . Noah, animals preserved . . . earth vastly
changed . . . God starts over with eight people.

19

Read Genesis 6

The LORD was grieved that he had made man on the earth, and his heart was filled with pain. So the LORD said, "I will wipe mankind, whom I have created, from the face of the earth—men and animals, and creatures that move along the ground, and birds of the air—for I am grieved that I have made them." But Noah found favor in the eyes of the LORD.

Genesis 6:6. 7

Third inning —
HISTORY'S BIGGEST RAINOUT

ON AUGUST 13, 1978, the Baltimore Orioles lost a 3-0 lead when New York exploded for five runs in the top of the seventh inning. Then heavy rains fell. The grounds crew deliberately took so long getting the tarp on the field that it became unplayable. The game was declared a rainout, the score reverted back to the last completed inning, and the Orioles won, 3-0!

A long time ago God once sent an even bigger rainout because mankind refused to turn to Him. He decided to wipe out His creation and revert back to the previous inning! Here's how it happened:

After Adam's sin in the Garden of Eden, things went from bad to worse. Children were born to Eve, some of whom trusted God and some of whom became very wicked. Eventually, they began to intermarry, as godly men fell prey to the attractiveness of beautiful but ungodly women. This "unequal yoke" drew men further from the Lord, so God limited their lifespans on earth (Genesis 6:1-3). Man's wickedness kept increasing and God saw that every inclination of his heart was "only evil all the time" (Genesis 6:5). So God decided to wipe out man, woman, and child with a great flood and start over. Yet, in His grace, He made a way of escape for all who would trust Him and value a relationship to Him. His means of grace was an ark and the man who found grace and extended it to others was Noah.

21

For the first time, God used the word "covenant" in dealing with man (Genesis 6:18). By His solemn, binding agreement, God promised to save all who would enter the ark to escape the coming flood. Only eight people accepted God's invitation (Genesis 7:13). The flood was brought about by a deluge of rain, plus an enormous upheaval of land and sea in a universal catastrophe.

No one knows the date of the flood, but we do know how long it lasted (Genesis 7:11, 8:14). After 40 days and nights of constant rain and the bursting forth of waters from the seas, water remained over the earth for 150 days (Genesis 7:14). Nothing lived, except those eight people and animals on the ark, and the sea creatures.

Convulsions of the earth (forming great mountain ranges and valleys), the pressure of such great amounts of water (forming coal from pressed, live plants), and the vast run-off and sedimentation (forming various layers of soil) greatly speeded up geologic processes. Great herds of elephants, numbering in the hundreds of thousands, have been found buried in frozen silt on high ground in Siberia, all over Asia, in Alaska, and in Canada. These animals were drowned! The silt froze and the mammoths were never unfrozen, as post-flood conditions were drastically changed.

God's judgment on sin was sure and complete. He tolerates man's evil deeds only for a time. History's first rainout destroyed all of creation except those eight people and the animals saved on the ark. Man lost that game, and there were no games played on the earth for quite some time!

Read Genesis 7

And Noah did all that the Lord commanded him.

Genesis 7:5

Third inning —
BY FAITH, NOAH . . .

ATHLETES DO MANY THINGS by faith, whether they realize it or not. A hitter can see a ball only so far to the plate before losing its location because his eyes can't work that fast. He actually swings where he thinks the ball will be, by faith. A fielder positions himself where he believes (based upon past experiences) the ball will be hit. He trusts the scouting report and the wisdom of his coaches. Even sitting in the dugout involves faith—faith that the bench will support one's weight! There is true faith only when it is demonstrated by swinging the bat, moving to a certain spot, or sitting down on the bench!

Noah demonstrated faith in a crucial period of history. In Hebrews 11:7, the writer says, "By faith Noah, when warned about things not yet seen, in holy fear built an ark to save his family. By his faith he condemned the world and became heir of the righteousness which comes by faith." It wasn't raining when Noah entered the ark. In fact, it had never rained before in history! The earth was watered by a mist from the ground (Genesis 2:5, 6). God had warned man that he had 120 years to repent before the flood would destroy the world because of its exceedingly wicked sin (Genesis 6:3).

Noah was no cave man. He was a very intelligent person and as he worked on the ark, building to God's exact specifications (450' long x 75' wide x 45' deep with three levels), he preached to anyone who would listen. God waited patiently for man to repent (1 Peter 3:20). Noah worked and preached by faith in the promises of

23

God—that He would save anyone who got into the ark and that a terrible judgment was coming.

God sent many signs, including the preaching of Noah, the translation (removal from the earth) of Enoch, who was a very Godly man (Hebrews 11:5, 6), and the life of Methuselah. Methuselah was the oldest man to ever live (969 years) and his name means "when he is dead it shall be sent." But despite all of God's warnings, man continued in rebellion against Him.

Finally, God sent the animals to Noah (v 9). Instinctively, they boarded the ark (even the animals knew trouble was coming)! It was God who shut the only door (v. 16) and sealed them in and all others out. For seven days not a drop of water fell (v 10). Then the "bottom fell out." Not one living thing on earth survived.

It was totally by faith that Noah built and boarded the ark. He trusted God and obeyed His Word. And it is by faith today that we are saved from the wrath to come. Jesus is the only "door," the only "ark," in which we must be saved. One day, God will "shut the door" of opportunity for repentance. Every person must decide now whether to trust God's Word or to reject it. What have you decided?

Read Genesis 8

But God remembered Noah and all the wild animals and the livestock that were with him in the ark, and he sent a wind over the earth, and the waters receded.

Genesis 8:1

Third inning —
GOD REMEMBERS

MAN IS A FORGETFUL CREATURE. On October 15, 1917, in the final game of the World Series, the Giants caught Chicago's Eddie Collins in a rundown betwen third and home. But pitcher Rube Benton forgot to cover home plate. When catcher Bill Rariden ran up the line and threw the ball to the third baseman, Collins ran home with a vital run as Chicago won, 4-2. Benton's forgetfulness hurt his team in a crucial situation.

God is not forgetful, though man often forgets even the most vital things. It's a good thing for all of us that He remembered Noah in the ark. The Bible says the flood waters covered everything on earth. The Ararat mountain range, where the ark came to rest, is 16,000 feet high (over 3 miles). It was a tremendous amount of water that God used when He opened up the subterranean stores and dumped the floodgates of heaven on the earth for 40 days and nights (7:11, 12). Every living thing that walked or flew was killed, except those people and animals saved in the ark.

By adding the days given in Genesis, we know that Noah spent 371 days aboard the ark. Genesis 8:1 says, "But God remembered Noah and all the wild animals, and the livestock that were with him in the ark, and he sent a wind over the earth, and the waters receded." It was not that God put those creatures on the ark, forgot about them for a year, and suddenly recalled what He had done. The word means He was "faithful" to Noah. He never left him. He didn't play a cruel trick on Noah for a year by abandoning the ship.

God does not forget you and me in our trials. He plays no cruel tricks on us. We are constantly on His mind. He is faithful to us, even when we don't feel like He is near. He knows our every need and circumstance and has not forgotten. He will deliver us in His time.

Read Genesis 9

I have set my rainbow in the clouds, and it will be a sign of the covenant between me and the earth.

Genesis 9:13

Third inning —
GOD'S SIGN IN THE CLOUDS

BASEBALL COACHES USE SIGNS to relay information. They tell players what to do or what not to do. The tip of the hat, touching a part of the body, or standing a certain way is a method of secretly relaying instructions to players.

God sent a sign to all creation very early in history. He put a rainbow in the sky after each rainstorm to remind us that He would never completely flood the earth again. Man needed to be reminded that God was interested in man's welfare and not his destruction, for great changes had taken place upon the earth after the flood waters receded. Not only was the topography of the land greatly altered by the rushing waters, but the four seasons of the year were initiated (Genesis 8:22). God put the fear of man in the animals (9:2) and permitted man to eat meat (9:3). To demonstrate the precious nature of human life, God established capital punishment (9:5, 6) and gave government the authority (and responsibility) to execute those who kill others. God put His rainbow (sign) in the sky to remind us that He promises never to flood the earth again (9:8-17). The next time He judges the earth it will be by fire (2 Peter 3). This "new agreement" has been called the "Noahic Covenant."

Yet, there are some remarkable similarities between the days immediately preceeding the flood and today. You see, the flood didn't change human nature. Even the eight people on the ark were sinners saved by grace.

27

God still said that "every inclination of man's heart is evil from childhood (8:21). Noah soon became drunk (9:21). Things have been degenerating since the flood. Years later, Jesus said, "As it was in the days of Noah, so it will be at the coming of the Son of Man" (Matthew 24:37). How was it in Noah's day? There was a tremendous population explosion. There was almost unrestrained evil behavior. People were preoccupied with their own affairs and were ignoring God. It sounds like the 1990s! Surely we are in the "bottom of the ninth inning." Jesus is coming soon to take over the rulership of this world and to judge the world! But because of God's sign, we know He won't flood the earth again. When He renovates the earth, He will use a different method. He does not desire that anyone perish, but that all repent of sin and be saved (2 Peter 3:9). Even so, come Lord Jesus!

Fourth inning —

ABRAHAM

The Real One . . .

JESUS CHRIST

Inning	1	2	3	4	5	6	7	8	9	10
SATAN	0	Fall	0	0						
GOD	Creation	Promise	Flood	Abraham						

How They Scored

Fourth inning —
God chooses Abraham . . . makes unconditional prom-
ises to him and his descendents . . . Abraham fails . . .
God is faithful . . . Isaac . . . Jacob becomes Israel.

29

Read Genesis 12

The LORD has said to Abram, "Leave your country, your people and your father's household and go to the land I will show you. I will make you into a great nation and I will bless you; I will make your name great, and you will be a blessing. I will bless those who bless you, and whoever curses you I will curse; and all peoples on earth will be blessed through you.

Genesis 12:1-3

Fourth inning —
God's Draft Pick

JOSH BOOTY is a Christian young man who attended a Christian school in Shreveport, Louisiana. He planned to accept a football/baseball scholarship to Louisiana State University in the fall of 1994. But the Florida Marlins made him their #1 draft choice in the spring and offered to reward him with 1.6 million dollars. Josh accepted the call and went to the minor leagues in hopes of a major league career some day.

God has a right to "draft" people just as professional teams draft players like Josh Booty. When God drafted Abraham, he was a prosperous, middle-aged idol-worshiper, firmly settled in an ungodly culture. The story is told in Genesis 12, a pivotal chapter in Scripture. McGee calls it the "hub of the Bible," for it is here that God turns from dealing with the whole world to dealing with one man through which to save the world.

After the flood, civilization again degenerated into brutal paganism. Ur of the Chaldees (Babylon) was Abraham's home (Acts 7:2-4). God promised Abraham (1) a great name, (2) a great nation, and (3) blessing for the world through him (Genesis 18:18, 22:18). Abraham was to leave friends, family, and a highly developed civilization and go to a place of which he knew nothing (Hebrews 11:8-10). His new home turned out to be 1500 miles away and among very barbaric people. Abraham obeyed, left home, and became the epitome of faith. James 2:20-24 says Abraham's faith was made complete by what he *did* and God counted his faith as righteousness (Romans 4:3; Galatians 3:6)!

All great men believe in something greater than themselves. Abraham became a great man because of his faith in God. He was of noble character, for we see how he gave preference to Lot during a dispute (Genesis 13). Abraham became the world's most famous man — just as God promised him a "great name." Millions of Jews, Moslems, and Christians who never heard of Willie Mays, Troy Aikman, or Shaquille O'Neal hold him in high esteem. God called him "my friend" (Isaiah 41:8).

Yet, even Abraham's faith didn't result in *complete* obedience. He took some of his extended family to Haran. He believed God, but he was a *weak* believer. He lied continually about Sarah, saying she was his sister. Sarah was very beautiful and was his half-sister, but she was also his wife and Abraham lied to save his own skin (12:12). Each time God miraculously overrode his mistakes and continued His sovereign plan! The Lord visited Abraham at least seven times to develop his faith. Though Abraham failed continually, God was faithful to His promise and plan to bless the world through him.

God also has "drafted" you, if you are a believer in Jesus Christ. He credits our faith in Jesus Christ as righteousness (Romans 4:18-25)! We are children of Abraham and children of God (Galatians 3:7-9)! He is as faithful to us as He was to Abraham.

Read Genesis 15

On that day the LORD made a covenant with Abram and said,
"To your descendants I give this land, from the river of Egypt
to the great river, the Euphrates —"

Genesis 15:18

Fourth inning —
ABRAHAM'S MULTI-YEAR CONTRACT

PROFESSIONAL ATHLETES and coaches seek the security of contracts spread over many years. The athletes know that one simple injury can spell the end of their playing days. The coaches need time to develop their own system. In 1994, Coach Ken Hatfield left Clemson because the administration refused to extend his contract. Ken knew that not being able to guarantee a recruit he would be his coach for all four years would hurt recruiting. So, he decided to seek other employment and ended up at Rice University.

In Genesis 15, God restated His covenant with Abraham. Not only did this plan encompass a vastly beautiful and prosperous land, but it was a "multi-year" agreement! In fact, it is to last forever! Talk about security! The Bible says, "Abram believed the Lord, and he credited it to him as righteousness" (v 6). Scripture repeats this principle many times (Romans 4:1-5; Galatians 3:6-9; James 2:23). The contract was signed and "notarized" by God Himself on the very same day. Legal procedure at the time was for two parties to split an animal in half, join hands, and walk between the halves together to signify their agreement (Jeremiah 34:18). In this special, multi-year, no-cut contract, God put Abraham into a deep sleep and the LORD Himself walked between the halves. A smoking firepot (His judgment) and a burning torch (His light) signified His presence. Abraham did nothing! He was asleep at the time! God "cut the deal," unconditionally guaranteeing the outcome because of the faith of Abraham.

33

What a picture of our salvation by faith in Jesus Christ! We are paralyzed in sin and can do nothing to merit salvation. If we had to promise anything (to keep the bargain) the contract would have been null and void because we *couldn't* keep our part of the deal! Jesus did all the work on the cross. He "cut the deal" and promises to save all who simply believe in Him. He "counts" us as righteous on the basis of faith when we are hell-deserving sinners! Like Abraham, we are saved not because of our faithfulness, but because of our faith in a wonderful Savior. Praise His Holy Name!

Read Genesis 16

So Hagar bore Abram a son, and Abram gave the name
Ishmael to the son she had borne.

Genesis 16:15

Fourth inning —
ABRAHAM FUMBLES THE BALL

NO GOOD FOOTBALL TEAM can turn the ball over
repeatedly and win. Sometimes, a mediocre team
fumbles so often it just seems to give the game away! On
September 13, 1980, East Carolina University lost the
most fumbles in one quarter in college football history —
five! When the Pirates fumbled on five straight possessions in the third quarter, Southwestern Louisiana
turned them into 24 points and a 27-21 victory.

Even God's choice servants are not immune from
"dropping the ball" on occasion. Let's examine the life of
the "father of faith," for example.

Abraham had been living in Canaan for 10 years. He
had enjoyed God's faithfulness, but so far had no son to
inherit his possessions or the promises of God. His wife,
though very beautiful, was barren. He had lied continually to keep her (Genesis 20:13), for without a son, God's
promised blessing upon his family was doomed. So
Sarah and Abraham decided to take matters into their
own hands.

The whole thing was Sarah's idea. She had an Egyptian maid-servant (probably obtained on their ill-advised
trip to Egypt years earlier) named Hagar. Sarah planned
to "loan" Hagar to Abraham, they were to have sex, and
the child would be the offspring of Abram so he could
inherit God's promises. After all, it was the culturally
accepted practice of the day. Eighty-six-year-old Abraham agreed to the plan to "help" God keep His promise!

Two wives under one roof always mean trouble.
When Hagar conceived, a rivalry was born. It culminated

35

in Sarah mistreating Hagar and sending her away. The Lord Jesus (God in the flesh) appeared to Hagar as she fled toward Egypt and made a promise that Ishmael (which means "God hears") would father a wild, nomadic people (Arabs) which would live among his brothers in the desert. Chapter 16 of Genesis records a real "fumble" of one of God's men of faith. While we would criticize the use of a concubine (God doesn't condone it either), the most serious sin of Abraham was that of unbelief in Almighty God and His ability to fulfill His promise.

Unbelief always complicates our lives. It was 13 more years before God appeared to Abraham with news of the son He would give him. The Arabs are hostile to Israel (and to each other) to this day! Abraham should have just believed God and trusted His timing instead of taking matters into his own hands. So should we!

Read Genesis 21:1-7

Now the LORD was gracious to Sarah as he had said, and the LORD did for Sarah what he had promised. Sarah became pregnant and bore a son to Abraham in his old age, at the very time God had promised him.

Genesis 21:1-2

Fourth inning —
GOD'S PROMISE FULFILLED

IN OCTOBER, 1993, Boston Red Sox management told coaches Rick Burleson, Al Bumbry, and Rich Gale that all three would be rehired for the 1994 season. Gale said he was told a new contract was in the mail. Yet, all three were fired three weeks after the season ended, as the general manager replaced them with coaches he had known previously! The three men felt that the promise of management was unfulfilled and they had to seek other jobs.

God's ways are not like man's ways. Unlike human management, He never goes back on His word, though sometimes it seems that His promises are delayed in being fulfilled so long that we begin to doubt them. But the birth of Isaac confirms to us that God always keeps His word. Twenty-five years ago, when Abraham was 75, God had promised him a son who would be his heir and who would be in the line of the coming Messiah. Despite Abraham's lack of trust at age 86 (when he took Hagar and fathered Ishmael), God did fulfill His promise. When Abraham was 100 and Sarah was 90 years old, God miraculously gave them Isaac (which means "laughter")! The child brought much joy to his parents and to those who knew them.

The birth of Isaac was strikingly similar to that of the Lord Jesus Christ. Both were promised long before they were born, both were miraculous, both brought joy to the father (Matthew 3:17), both came at God's appointed time (Galatians 4:4), and both boys were obedient unto death (Genesis 22). Most importantly, both prove that God is faithful to keep His promises. He is absolutely trustworthy. If He says He'll do something, He is bound to keep His word. We must wait patiently for Him to act instead of acting on our own, for He always moves at just the right time.

Read Genesis 32

So Jacob was left alone, and a man wrestled with him until daybreak . . . Then the man said, "Your name will no longer be Jacob, but Israel, because you have struggled with God and with men and have overcome."

Genesis 21:24, 28

Fourth inning —
History's Most Famous Wrestling Match

A BIZARRE HIGH SCHOOL wrestling match took place on January 28, 1982 in the state of Washington. White Swan High School had only six wrestlers, while Highland High School had only five. But none of the White Swan wrestlers was in the same weight class as any of the Highland boys. So, every match was declared a forfeit and White Swan won 36-30 because it had one extra man!

Another bizarre wrestling match was once held at the Jabbok River. Because of its eternal significance, let's examine it closely. This incidence takes place many years after Abraham's death at age 175. His son Isaac has fathered twin sons — Jacob and Esau. Esau had forfeited his rights as elder son because of his disinterest in leadership of the family (Genesis 25:33-34). God's promise of a great nation and a Messiah is to be fulfilled through Jacob. There was cunning, treachery, and infighting throughout the family and Jacob (which means "schemer") lived up to his name. It was God Himself who was to change his nature. He used a wrestling match to do it!

Jacob was returning to Canaan after years of exile in Haran. When he paused at the Jabbok River to spend the night, a man confronted him. All night they wrestled! Finally, the man "touched" Jacob's thigh, dislocating it. Jacob realized he was wrestling someone more powerful than himself, but would still not let go. He asked for a blessing and received it.

39

It was the Lord Jesus Himself who showed Jacob his weakness in his own efforts. Jesus brought down Jacob's self-sufficient pride and redirected his will to win, to achieve, to excel, to obtain for himself. From that time on, Jacob was changed. He still sinned, but he clung to the Lord like a drowning man clings to a life preserver. He realized his only hope was for God to bless him. God changed Jacob's name to <u>Israel</u> (which means "God strives"). He had clung to the One who held him in his desperate hour, and was made fit to inherit the promise of blessing for the entire world! Years later, Hosea used Jacob's persistence in prayer as an example to the entire nation. Hosea 12:4 says, "He struggled with the angel and overcame him; he wept and begged for his favor." How they needed to return to Him!

It was through Israel that God sent His Son, born of a woman, to die for the sins of man and to set us free! God loves it when we cling to Him, recognizing our weakness. If we will hold on to the One who desires to change us into His image, He will bless us! Let us hold on, persisting in prayer until the blessing is given and received.

Fifth inning —

ISRAEL BECOMES A NATION

The Real One . . .

JESUS CHRIST

Inning	1	2	3	4	5	6	7	8	9	10
SATAN	0	Fall	0	0	Slavery					
GOD	Creation	Promise	Flood	Abraham	Israel					

How They Scored

Fifth inning —
God gives Joseph a dream . . . Satan tries to destroy him
. . . slavery in Egypt . . . Israel multiples in slavery . . .
God delivers them through Moses . . . Israel learns God
is trustworthy . . . God gives His law for their good.

Read Genesis 37

Joseph had a dream, and when he told it to his brothers, they hated him all the more.

Genesis 37:5

. . . and they took him and threw him into the cistern.

Genesis 37:24

. . . his brothers pulled Joseph up out of the cistern and sold him for twenty shekels of silver to the Ishmaelites, who took him to Egypt.

Genesis 37:28

Fifth inning —
JOSEPH'S "UNCONDITIONAL RELEASE"

DAVE STEWART has no fond memories of Philadelphia. Traded from Texas to the Phillies in 1985, he was given up on and released after only 12 games in Philly in 1985-86. Since that time, Dave's career has been rejuvenated and he has pitched outstanding ball for Oakland and Toronto. When his baseball life seemed over, it was resurrected by teams that knew better how to use him.

Like an athlete who is no longer wanted, Joseph (Jacob's son) was given his "unconditional release" by his own brothers. The story is told in Genesis 37. For the remainder of the book, Joseph is the central figure. In fact, more chapters are devoted to the life of Joseph than to anyone else in Genesis.

Jacob favored Joseph over his other eleven sons. He gave him a colorful coat when he was 17 years old. The brothers were extremely resentful and had nothing kind to say to him. When God gave Joseph a dream of leadership and authority, they were even *more* spiteful. After his second dream, they hated his guts!

When Jacob sent Joseph to check on their welfare as they grazed his flocks, the brothers threw him into a dry cistern. Then, seeing a caravan of Arabs headed for Egypt, they sold him into slavery for 20 shekels of silver.

43

Finally, they killed a goat, dipped Joseph's coat in the blood, and showed it to Jacob. Jacob was tricked into believing a wild animal had devoured his son and he went into deep mourning.

No one else in all Scripture represents Jesus Christ more closely in character and in experience than Joseph. Both were especially loved by their fathers, both were hated and rejected, both made unusual claims, both were "slain" by their brothers, and both became a blessing to their people and to the whole world. It all started with rejection and an "unconditional release." But like Dave Stewart, God resurrected Joseph's career. And He raised Jesus from the dead. He can do the same for you!

Read Genesis 39

The Lord was with Joseph and he prospered, and he lived in the house of his Egyptian master.

Genesis 39:2

Fifth inning —
Joseph: Blessed of God

MICHAEL JORDON'S basketball success is well-known. He was a dominant player who became a fan favorite. But Michael is also an outstanding golfer. And after his first basketball career, his baseball skills were good enough to land a minor league contract. When he returned to basketball, he seemed to never miss a beat. It seems like Jordon is blessed by God in every sport he attempts.

The life of Joseph is the story of the blessing of God during both suffering and prosperity. After being sold, Joseph had an iron collar put around his neck and shackles put on his feet for the long trip into slavery (Psalm 105:17-18). He was sold to Potiphar, an official of Pharaoh in Egypt. But God was with Joseph all the way. He had a higher purpose for Joseph's life than could be seen with physical eyes.

Joseph served faithfully in Potiphar's house until framed by the man's adulterous wife. He was unjustly imprisoned and spent a total of 13 years as slave and prisoner (Genesis 39-41). Finally, through his interpretation of Pharaoh's dreams, Joseph was made prime minister of Egypt. Eventually, it was to Joseph that his brothers made reverent appeal for food, fulfilling all his God-given dreams! Jacob came to Egypt and the family was reunited and prospered.

Joseph is the link between the *family* of Israel and the *nation* of Israel. Though he was righteous, he was not exempt from suffering. His faith was greatly tested. But God used him to get his people away from the evil influence of the Canaanites and to preserve their lives in a fruitful land while He judged them with famine. In fact, the wisdom of Joseph in storing grain saved the world. For 400 years, Israel stayed in Egypt while God gave the Amorites (in Canaan) a chance to turn to Him (Genesis 15:16). Israel was to become a great nation. Joseph could truthfully say to his brothers, "You intended to harm me, but God intended it for good, to accomplish what is now being done, the saving of many lives" (Genesis 50:20).

Read Exodus 12

*The blood will be a sign for you on the houses where you are;
and when I see the blood, I will pass over you. No destructive
plague will touch you when I strike Egypt.*

Exodus 12:13

Fifth inning
GOD'S WINDUP AND DELIVERY

A GOOD WIND-UP ENABLES a pitcher to remain bal-
anced and to deliver a pitch with efficiency. All waste
motion must be eliminated and full attention given to
throwing the baseball with accuracy. The delivery is the
culmination of a good wind-up.

Around 1445 B.C., God brought events to the point of
delivering the nation Israel from slavery in Egypt and
back into their land. These events are recorded in the
book of Exodus. Jacob's family had prospered in Egypt
until a new Pharaoh who knew nothing about Joseph
came to power (Exodus 1). The Israelites cried out to
God in their hard labor and the Lord sent them a deliv-
erer named Moses. Exodus 2-12 tells of Moses' birth, his
mistakes in trying to do things his own way, his call,
and the plagues God sent on the Egyptians to cause
them to release Israel. Chapters 12-14 are the climax of
that deliverance when all other plagues failed to soften
the heart of Pharaoh. These words describe God's
method of releasing His people and His complete destruction of the Egyptian army in the Red Sea. Though a
world power at the time, Egypt has *never* been the same
since that day!

Let's examine God's method of deliverance. Every
Israelite household was to take a year-old lamb without
defect, observe it for four days, and slaughter it at twi-
light on the 14th day of the month. Blood of the lamb
was to be placed on the sides and tops of the door
frames of each house and the roasted lamb was to be
eaten that same night. Bitter herbs and unleavened

47

bread were to be eaten. None was to be left over. This "Passover" meal was to be eaten with the cloak tucked into the belt, sandals on, and staff in hand. It was to be eaten quickly. They were to be ready to move out f-a-s-t!

The ceremony was to be duplicated throughout history as a reminder of how God struck the Egyptians and delivered His people. For seven days, the Passover would be observed (Exodus 12:14-20). As leaven symbolized the contamination of Egyptian slavery, the unleavened bread symbolized purity and freedom.

Israel obeyed (v 28)! Each family put the blood on the doorpost! At midnight, the Lord destroyed the firstborn of every household in Egypt — except those who had the blood applied (vs 29-30). Loud wailing was heard all over Egypt! One of history's largest mass funerals was in process. The remaining Egyptians asked Israel to leave immediately! They now feared for their own lives! After 430 years, Israel was finally free! Possibly up to five million people departed, delivered not by Moses, but by the blood of the lamb!

There was no other way out of Egypt but God's way! Israel could not have fought her way out against this world power. It had to be God's way of deliverance or no way. And there is no other way of being saved from our sin but God's way. Jesus, our Passover Lamb, is God's way. Like the lamb, He was "observed" (questioned) for four days before being crucified in Jerusalem over 1400 years later. His blood must be "sprinkled upon the doorposts of our hearts." The escape from slavery is a great picture of our escape from sin. Have you trusted God's Son and been delivered? You can be.

Read Exodus 14

And when the Israelites saw the great power the Lord dis-
played against the Egyptians, the people feared the LORD and
put their trust in him and in Moses his servant.

Exodus 14:31

Fifth inning —
LEARNING TO TRUST GOD

PROFESSIONAL SPORTS TEAMS are owned by men
whose goal is to make money. They move franchises on
that basis, even after promising fans the opposite. In
1957, Brooklyn Dodgers' owner Walter O'Malley devas-
tated Brooklyn fans when he moved the Dodgers to Los
Angeles after promising fans the team would not abandon them. Fans were hurt and angry at the betrayal.
Robert Irsay did the same thing with the Baltimore Colts
football team. On March 29, 1984, at 12:17 am, he tried
to avoid local protest by loading moving vans with the
team's equipment and moving to Indianapolis under
cover of darkness. When Colt's fans awoke, they had no
team!

Our God is not like human owners of professional
teams. As Exodus 14 reveals, He is fully trustworthy.
This chapter tells the story of the most memorable event
in Israel's history. It is the story of the nation's deliverance from the Egyptian army and the destruction of that
powerful military force in the Red Sea. Here's how it
happened:

Pharaoh's heart had remained hard even when he let
Israel leave his country. He quickly changed his mind
and pursued them with all his chariots, including 600 of
his best military vehicles (v 7). Trapped "between the
devil and the deep, blue sea," Israel was terrified, perplexed, confused, and frustrated. They cried out to God,
but didn't trust Him even as they cried out! Fear dis-
torted their memories of deliverance from slavery and
they accused Moses of leading them to their deaths.

49

But God was behind their circumstances. His purpose was to gain glory through Pharaoh (vs 17-18) and He quickly delivered His people. The angel of the Lord and a cloud came between the army of Egypt and Israel. Using Moses' faith (the people had none) to part the Red Sea, God led Israel on dry ground to safety!

When Pharaoh's army pursued, God released the walls of water and drowned every man and beast! Even the Egyptians recognized the supernatural miracle of God that led to their deaths (v 25). As their bodies washed up to shore, Israel broke out in praise and worship (chapter 15).

Israel was never the same (v 31). Though they had many "ups and downs" (Psalms 105-106) they now feared God and trusted Moses' leadership. They were "baptized into Moses" (1 Corinthians 10:1-2). In other words, the nation was *identified* with Moses and *separated* from their old lives under Egyptian authority.

Crossing the Red Sea is a picture of our salvation from sin. We identify with Jesus Christ as they identified with Moses' leadership. We leave the slavery of the world (Egypt) for the freedom of following Jesus. He did all the work to save us by dying on the cross. We must simply trust Him!

Read Exodus 20

Moses said to the people, "Do not be afraid. God has come to test you, so that the fear of God will be with you to keep you from sinning."

Exodus 20:20

Fifth Inning
KNOWING THE RULES

COACHES AND PLAYERS are sometimes at a disadvantage if they don't know all the rules of the game. A good coach spends some time to learn what the rulebook says. In 1929, Dutch Clark won a 3-2 football game for Colorado because he knew the rules. As time expired and his team was behind 2-0, Clark drop-kicked a 20-yard field goal against Denver University. The official signaled wide and stated, "The ball went over the goal post." Dutch asked the official to repeat his statement and then he appealed to the other officials. They agreed that any ball going over the post is good, changed the call, and gave Colorado a 3-2 victory! It all happened because a player knew the rules.

The Israelites needed a standard to understand God's rules, just as an athletic team needs a rulebook. Exodus 20 explains the giving of the Ten Commandments — the first part of the law — to provide that standard. God gave the commandments to Moses on stone tablets. The first four commandments reveal our duty to God:

1. "You shall have no other gods before (besides) me." There is only one God and man is to worship nothing or no one else. Anything to which you give mind, heart, and soul easily becomes your god.

2. "You shall not make for yourself an idol . . ." The essence of God is spiritual and unseen, so we are not to use any visual portrayals of God or His creation in worship. No visual idols can possibly portray Him. He is very jealous, so we dare not set our affections upon any other gods.

51

3. "You shall not misuse the name of the LORD your God." We must not use God's name in swearing (God's last name is not "damn"), or with a flippant attitude, or to accomplish a selfish or wicked goal.

4. "Remember the Sabbath day by keeping it holy." This law was a reminder of God's rest after creating the universe. God did not need rest, but man needs to be reminded of God's greatness by setting time apart unto Him.

The last six commandments reveal our duty to each other:

5. "Honor your father and your mother." This is a measure of how godly we really are! A promise of long life follows this law!

6. "You shall not murder." Life and death are in the hands of God and He forbids an individual taking another's life (murder). This command has nothing to do with a nation waging a just war or protecting life by executing criminals.

7. "You shall not commit adultery." God wants to preserve homes and family relationships. Sex outside of marriage is always wrong.

8. "You shall not steal." God respects human property and commands man to do the same.

9. "You shall not give false testimony against your neighbor." God is truthful and expects the same of us. This protects a person's name or reputation.

10. "You shall not covet . . . anything that belongs to your neighbor." This deals with our attitude of gain at the expense of others. We must be content with what God provides. Covetousness is idolatry (Colossians 3:5).

Why did God give these Ten Commandments? First, they reveal His nature. His character is revealed in what God expects of man . Secondly, these laws reveal our human depravity and inability to save ourselves (Romans 3:20). Romans 7:7 says, "Indeed I would not have known what sin was except through the law." Galatians 3:24 says, "So the law was put in charge to lead us to Christ that we might be justified by faith." The law and an altar go together, just as a mirror accompanies a bathroom sink. The law reveals sin and on the altar a blood sacrifice covers sin. The mirror reveals the uncleanness and one washes in the sink. The law is the mirror and Jesus' blood shed on the altar (cross) cleanses all who are washed in it! How we thank God for revealing both Himself and our sin by His holy law, and then for sending Jesus to pay for the sin and lead us back to Himself!

Sixth inning —

ISRAEL: FROM RAGS TO RICHES . . . AND BACK TO RAGS

The Real One . . .

JESUS CHRIST

Inning	1	2	3	4	5	6	7	8	9	10
SATAN	0	Fall	0	0	Slavery	Captivity				
GOD	Creation	Promise	Flood	Abraham	Israel	David				

How They Scored

Sixth inning —
Israel wavers in trusting God . . . God holds on to them. . . Moses predicts a great prophet is coming . . . Joshua leads Israel into the Promised Land . . . the nation stumbles again, adopting the practices of pagan cultures. . . God chooses King David to lead the nation . . . civil war . . . taken into captivity and finally returned to the land.

55

Read Deuteronomy 9

It is not because of your righteousness or your integrity that you are going in to take possession of their land; but on account of the wickedness of these nations, the LORD your God will drive them out before you, to accomplish what he swore to your fathers, to Abraham, Isaac and Jacob. Understand, then, that it is not because of your righteousness that the LORD your God is giving you this good land to possess, for you are a stiffnecked people.

Deuteronomy 9:5, 6

Sixth Inning —
GOD'S FAITHFULNESS IN OUR INCONSISTENCIES

MITCH WILLIAMS had an up and down career. He earned the nickname "Wild Thing" by his terribly inconsistent control on the mound. Mitch had a great 1993 season, saving 45 games for the Phillies. But his terrible post-season led to a trade to the Astros. Before the 1994 season was over, Mitch had been released by the Astros because of his inconsistency and ineffectiveness. He never regained enough control to become an effective big league pitcher.

The nation of Israel had been more inconsistent than Mitch Williams! After 40 years of wandering in the desert because of unbelief, Israel finally was ready to enter the Promised Land — Canaan. They had been unfaithful to God, flunking every test He had sent to them. Now, they faced wicked enemies which were stronger than themselves (v 2). The Canaanites had superior physical strength, fortifications, weapons, experience, and numbers. Humanly speaking, conquering the land was impossible.

But God is a wise manager. He gave them victory anyway! He delights in lost causes. Overwhelming odds are his forte! It was not because they were righteous people, because they had material possessions or because they were smarter that the Lord helped them. God gave Israel the land to show the Canaanites that his patience with sin does expire and to demonstrate to Israel that He is a faithful God. God called his people "stiff-necked" — slow to bow down to Him. It was only through Moses' faithful prayer and fasting for 40 days on their behalf that God didn't wipe them out and start over (v 14). The nation had rebelled against God at Kadesh Barnea, refusing to trust Him when He told them to enter the land the first time. Therefore, He let them wander until the older generation died and He took their children into the land. He demonstrated His trustworthiness by fulfilling his ancient promises to Abraham, Isaac, and Jacob that their descendants would inhabit the land.

What does God expect from His people? He expects us to fear Him, to walk with Him, to serve Him, and to obey Him (Deuteronomy 10:12, 13). Was Israel obedient? No way! Did they suffer for their disobedience? Yes! Did God abandon them? No! He is faithful, even when we are as inconsistent as Mitch Williams' control on the mound (2 Timothy 2:13)! God does not save us because we are good. He is in the business of saving bad people who acknowledge their sin and turn to Him. All who have been saved have recognized His faithfulness in spite of their own failures! What a wonderful God we have!

Read Deuteronomy 18:9-22

The Lord your God will raise up for you a prophet like me from among your own brothers. You must listen to him.

Deuteronomy 18:15

Sixth Inning —
A MANAGER WORTH LISTENING TO

EARL WEAVER was not known as the greatest player during his 13 minor league seasons. But it was as a manager that his talent shined. In 1956, he was a second baseman when he replaced his manager in Knoxville to start his managerial career. In July, 1968, Earl replaced Hank Bauer as Baltimore Orioles' manager, finished in second place, and won three straight pennants from 1969-1971. He managed Baltimore into the '80s and became known as a genius for his handling of men, judge of talent, and attention to detail. No one had a keener knowledge of pitchers. Earl Weaver was a first-class manager.

God provided his people with a first-class manager (Moses) when He led them out of Egypt. But before they entered the promised land, Moses died. Before he died, he predicted the future arrival of a great "manager," one to whom they *must* listen.

Moses predicted this prophet (like himself) would one day be sent to teach the people, to deliver them from their enemies, to give them guidance in life, and to intercede for them before God the Father. Moses had done all these things, but a Prophet greater than Moses was to come! Israel was directed by Moses to listen to Him.

Deuteronomy 18:15 is the most clear promise of a great leader in all the law of Moses, and Jesus Christ is the clear fulfillment of this prophecy (Acts 3:19-23, 7:37). When most of Israel refused to believe Jesus, He said, "Your accuser is Moses, on whom your hopes are

59

set. If you believed Moses, you would believe me, for he wrote about me" (John 5:46)! The religious people of Jesus' day crucified the Prophet sent by Jehovah to guide them! A minority of the people recognized Him as the Prophet Moses predicted (John 6:14).

To which "manager" (prophet) are you listening? There are many conflicting voices in this world. Where do you obtain guidance? Like the Canaanites, many people in America use drugs, astrology, witchcraft, and contact with demons to find enlightenment and power. But true guidance comes only from Jesus Christ. Every other source of information and help is a lie. Are you being led by God's true Prophet?

Read Joshua 1

Have I not commanded you? Be strong and courageous. Do not be terrified; do not be discouraged, for the Lord your God will be with you wherever you go.

Joshua 1:9

Sixth inning —
JOSHUA: STAYING ON THE OFFENSIVE

JOE LEWIS was one of the greatest heavyweight boxers of all time. One day he was asked, "What is the secret of your success?" Lewis said that he always studied each opponent thoroughly and, as a result, he was seldom surprised and was able to stay on the offensive throughout the entire fight.

Possessing the Promised Land involved the same "attack mode" that Joe Lewis used in boxing. God's people had to stay on the offensive. But Israel's hero (Moses) was dead. The nation was still not in the land when God appointed Joshua to succeed him. Joshua was to lead Israel in the annihilation of the Canaanites and to possess the 300,000 square miles of promised land. All was to be accomplished by faith in the power of God. But Joshua needed encouragement to put his faith in God and to stay on the offensive for God.

The countryside in Palestine was full of people who had no use for God. The Canaanites used child sacrifice to "manipulate" events of their lives by "forcing" their gods into looking kindly upon them. They were heavily into witchcraft, drug usage (sorcery), and attempts to contact the dead — all for the purpose of obtaining guidance or enlightenment. After many years of warning, with an open door to come to the true and living God, the Lord's patience ran out. God gave Israel the land and commanded the extermination of the Canaanites. He knew their detestable practices could be picked up even by His own people.

61

Years earlier, Joshua and Caleb had voiced confidence in God's ability to give Israel the promised land (Numbers 13-14). Only these two of the 12 sent to spy out the land had any faith in God, despite overwhelming odds against them. They were the only two spies who lived through the 40 years of desert wanderings. Now, they were to trust God to give them the land He had promised.

The God of all comfort (2 Corinthians 1:3, 4) offered encouragement to Joshua. Three times God says, "Be strong and courageous." He promises never to leave or forsake Joshua. In Hebrew, God literally says, "I will not be weak towards you." Joshua is to succeed in all he will do. Personal courage, complete obedience, and meditation on the Word of God (vs 7, 8) are the ingredients for his success. Joshua must not be afraid to step out in faith, must do exactly as God tells him, and must keep God's written Word constantly in his mind. He is promised prosperity and success in his mission as a result.

Even though God promised Joshua success, He didn't tell Joshua to sit back and do nothing! Joshua was to be aggressively pursuing the will of God. He was to place no faith in his own efforts independent of God, nor was he to be diverted in his focus. He was not to fill his mind with negative thoughts, but with the Word of God. As a keen military general, Joshua promptly sent spies into the land (Chapter 2). He obeyed God's instruction for taking Jericho (Chapter 5). He was elevated in the opinion of all Israel (3:7, 4:14) and feared throughout Canaan (6:27). He became the man God used to give Israel the land He promised to give them.

What "land" has God given you to possess? He has promised us all spiritual blessings in Christ. He said, "Be strong and courageous." Every place you go under His leading you are to succeed. Only remember to stay on the offensive, to obey His directions, and to fill your mind with His Word. He wants you to be prosperous and successful! He gains the victory and you will obtain deliverance and possessions!

Read Judges 2

The angel of the LORD went up from Gilgal to Bokim and said, "I brought you up out of Egypt and led you into the land that I swore to give to your forefathers. I said, 'I will never break my covenant with you, and you shall not make a covenant with the people of this land, but you shall break down their altars.' Yet you have disobeyed me. Why have you done this?"

Judges 2:1, 2

Sixth inning —

THE ROCKY ROAD
OF INCOMPLETE OBEDIENCE

WHEN REGGIE JACKSON signed a free agent contract with the Yankees in 1976, he didn't know he'd spend five rocky years squabbling with owner George Steinbrenner and manager Billy Martin. Reggie and the Yankees won four division titles, three American League pennants, and two World Championships as he became known as "Mr. October" for his clutch World Series performances. But the accompanying turmoil within the team always cast the organization in a dim light. Things never seemed to be quite like they could have been.

Despite achieving victory after victory, Israel and God had the same up and down relationship as Reggie and his bosses. Because they allowed some of the Canaanite tribes to co-exist among them, Israel was plagued with their false gods and the resulting warfare. The next generation of Israelites didn't remember what God had done for their fathers (vs 10-15). They forsook God, plunging into the idol-worship of Canaan. They became weak, easy prey for enemy raiders whom they had allowed to live among them. When Israel repented, the LORD raised up leaders called "judges" (military heroes) who would deliver them (v 16). Othniel, Deborah, Gideon, and Samson are the most well-known people God used to give Israel peace between cycles of oppression and war. Repeating cycles of disobedience, defeat, repentance, and deliverance continued for 350 years during this period of the "judges." Finally, God said He would no longer drive out the evil nations among the Israeli, but would use them to test His people to see whether they would walk in His ways (v 22). It was a frustrating period in history, as they alternately stopped trusting God, suffered, repented, were restored, and again stopped trusting God! Though the nation remained God's selected people, they suffered much grief because of their disobedience.

Christian, how is your walk with the Lord? Do you trust Him in all circumstances, even those you don't understand? Are you learning from the Israelites that when you stop trusting God and disobey or incompletely obey Him, the fear and oppression of the enemy (Satan) overtakes you? God has not changed. He is trustworthy. Remember His past help! You are still His child. He wants to deliver you from fear and turmoil. You don't need to continue along the rocky road of incomplete obedience. Keep your eyes upon Him and He will deliver you again.

Read 2 Samuel 7

Now then, tell my servant David, "This is what the Lord Almighty says: 'I took you from the pasture and from following the flock to be ruler over my people Israel. I have been with you wherever you have gone, and I have cut off all your enemies from before you. Now I will make your name great, like the names of the greatest men of the earth.'"

2 Samuel 7:8, 9

Sixth inning —
DAVID —TOUGH TO STAY ON TOP

IT'S HARD TO WIN a championship, but it's even harder to stay on top. Everyone is "gunning" for the team at the top. Complacency can set in as a team forgets how difficult it was to get to the pinnacle of success. Maybe that's why there are so few sports dynasties today.

Israel wanted a king (1 Samuel 8:4, 5). They first chose Saul, an impressive-looking man of physical stature (1 Samuel 9). He failed miserably. The book of 2 Samuel tells how God chose David, a shepherd boy who had learned to love and trust God (Chapter 5). No king of Israel was blessed like David. He reigned for 40 years (2 Samuel 5:4) and He was not ashamed to boldly worship the LORD (Chapter 6). David experienced great victories (Chapter 8). He did what was just and right, as he surrounded himself with Godly people (8:15-18). David was a great man and a great king.

But David was also a sinner. At the height of his power, David committed adultery with the beautiful Bathsheba and murdered her husband (Chapter 11). Though he repented, David suffered greatly. Civil war rocked his family and his kingdom. David had to flee from his capitol city (Jerusalem). God restored him to leadership, but David sinned again by numbering his soldiers (Chapter 24). He repented again and the judgment of God was stopped. The Bible says that David was a man after God's own heart (1 Samuel 13:14) despite his failures.

As history unfolded, many other kings took the throne of Israel. Some were good, some were very bad. Under evil leadership, the people forsook God. He used foreign powers (Assyria and Babylon) to remove most of the nation from the Promised Land. Then He brought them back. Finally, God sent His own Son, Jesus Christ, to occupy David's throne. Jesus was called the "Son of David" (Matthew 21:9). In the New Testament, King David is mentioned 59 times! But the Son of David was despised and rejected! Israel crucified her own King! But God raised Him from the dead! God's sovereign plan was being developed. Salvation from sin was made possible for everyone by King Jesus' death and resurrection! While earthly kings require subjects to die for them, King Jesus died for His subjects! One day He will finally sit on David's throne (Isaiah 9:7; Luke 1:32, 33) ruling not only Israel, but the entire world! You can be part of His kingdom by putting your faith in His sacrifice on the cross to take away your sins. Have you trusted King Jesus? Unlike King David, He sits at the top and He will never fall!

Seventh inning —

MESSIAH
THE SON OF DAVID

The Real One . . .

JESUS CHRIST

Inning	1	2	3	4	5	6	7	8	9	10
SATAN	0	Fall	0	0	Slavery	Captivity	Crucifixion			
GOD	Creation	Promise	Flood	Abraham	Israel	David	Resurrection			

How They Scored

Seventh inning —
God sent His Son, born of a virgin by the Holy Spirit . . . Satan tried to kill him continually . . . Finally, he was rejected and crucified . . . He rose from the dead three days later, appearing to hundreds of people . . . He returned to Heaven and will one day judge the world.

67

Read Matthew 1

But after he had considered this, an angel of the LORD appeared to him in a dream and said, "Joseph son of David, do not be afraid to take Mary home as your wife, because what is conceived in her is from the Holy Spirit. She will give birth to a son, and you are to give him the name Jesus, because he will save his people from their sins.

Matthew 1:20, 21

Seventh inning —
JESUS: SON OF DAVID, SON OF GOD

IN 1904, THE TENNESSEE VOLUNTEERS used a rather unorthodox maneuver to defeat Alabama. Fullback Sam McAllester wore a leather belt with loops sewn on each hip. On one 50-yard drive, Sam took a hand-off and two other backs each grabbed a loop and hurled him five yards over the line! Tennessee used the play repeatedly on the drive, finally throwing McAllester into the end zone for the game's only touchdown! Of course, the rules were later changed to eliminate such strategy.

Israel had been faithless and couldn't hear from God. For 400 years (between the Old and New Testaments) God waited for the perfect time to communicate with His people again. When He did speak, it was in a most unorthodox way! Matthew tells how He did it.

Choosing an engaged teenager (Mary), God made her pregnant by the power of the Holy Spirit. He used an angel to calm her fiancee's fears of her infidelity and to command Joseph to marry her and to raise the Son of God!

Jesus Christ had no earthly father! He was the Son of God. Matthew chapter 1 records the genealogy of Joseph, who was a descendent of King David. So, Jesus was also a "Son of David" and is legally entitled to the throne of Israel! Jesus was also a "Son of Abraham" (Matthew 1:1), and is the one through whom the whole world will be blessed. Luke 1:32, 33 records more of the angel's message to Mary: "Do not be afraid, Mary, you have found favor with God. You will be with child and will give birth to a son, and you are to give him the name Jesus. He will be great and will be called the Son of the Most High. The Lord God will give him the throne of his father David, and he will reign over the house of Jacob forever; his kingdom will never end."

Jesus was born, lived among men, taught His kingdom principles, and died for the sins of mankind. To atone for man's sins, Jesus had to be human. To live sinlessly and to be able to forgive sin, He had to be God. The virgin birth was the means God used to accomplish both!

God raised Jesus from the dead and He is coming back to take the throne of David to rule both Israel and the world. At that time, He will fulfill another prophecy: "Therefore God exalted him to the highest place and gave him the name that is above every name, that at the name of Jesus every knee should bow, in heaven and on earth and under the earth, and every tongue confess that Jesus Christ is Lord, to the glory of God the Father" (Philippians 2:9-11).

Read Matthew 26

The high priest said to him, "I charge you under oath by the living God: Tell us if you are the Christ, the Son of God." "Yes, it is as you say," Jesus replied. "But I say to all of you: In the future you will see the Son of Man sitting at the right hand of the Mighty One and coming on the clouds of heaven."

Matthew 26:63, 64

Seventh inning —
The Savior Is Rejected

ON JANUARY 3, 1994, in an AFC wild card play-off, the Houston Oilers blew a 35-3 third-quarter lead and lost 41-38 to the Buffalo Bills on Steve Christie's 32-yard field goal in overtime. It was the greatest comeback in NFL history. Or, it could be called the greatest "choke (by Houston) in NFL history. Either way, it was most unbelievable!

When God sent the Messiah to Israel for their national good, they did an equally unbelievable thing. They "choked" on their own Savior! After all His miracles of healing the sick and raising the dead, after His graceful teaching about the coming kingdom (the only bright spot in a dark world), and after hearing and understanding His claims, the nation of Israel rejected Him! They said, "no" to the very Son of God, whom Jehovah had promised to send for centuries!

The religious leaders didn't like it that Jesus was a friend to sinners (Matthew 9:10-13, 11:14). They expected Him to condemn, but He came to save from condemnation by offering His life in the place of us guilty sinners. They were jealous of His popularity among the common people. He replaced their religious racket with a personal relationship and they despised Him for it. Yet, when they tried to seize Him, no one could lay a hand on Him until He allowed them (John 7:25-32).

The LORD predicted His own rejection (v 2). He was

71

not surprised to be betrayed by Judas, nor was He shocked at Peter's denial of knowing Him. Jesus knew all things, including the heart of man. He knew why He had come to earth: to die on the cross as our substitute. He knew the horrors of torture and crucifixion and, though dreading it, His love for us overshadowed His agony and grief.

The Buffalo Bills made an unbelievable comeback against the Oilers. But even more unbelievable is the way Israel rejected the very hope of the nation and of the world! From Adam to Abraham to Moses, through King David and the prophets — all God had done had pointed toward Jesus Christ. And He was despised and rejected, a man of sorrows and grief as predicted by Isaiah (Isaiah 53). How unbelievably sinful and foolish we are!

Read John 8:12-59

"I tell you the truth," Jesus answered, "before Abraham was born, I am!" At this, they picked up stones to stone him, but Jesus hid himself, slipping away from the temple grounds.
John 8:58, 59

Seventh inning —
Liar, Lunatic, or Lord?

MANY COLLEGE FOOTBALL TEAMS lay claim to the #1 ranking as the season progresses each fall. Each week, polls of coaches and writers rank teams according to their own personal opinions. Even after the bowl games, teams continue to claim the top ranking. Probably even a playoff system would never put all claims to rest.

Jesus Christ left no doubt about who He claimed to be and what He came to do. He claimed to be the "light of the world" (v 12). Light is very complicated. We don't totally understand it. It is also absolutely essential. We can't live without light. The religious leaders rejected the light and their hostility against Him mounted. God the Father had spoken out of Heaven that Jesus was His Son (Mark 9:7). Still, the religious crowd rejected Him.

Jesus claimed God as His Father (v 18). Then He claimed to be the way to know the Father (v 19). He claimed to be from another world, a world above this one (v 23). He claimed to be the only way of salvation from sin (v 24). He claimed to be the Son of God who could set men free from sin (vs 31-36). He claimed to be sinless (v 46) and He was the only man to ever live who could back that claim with a perfect life! Because the Jews had no answer for Him, they ridiculed Him. They hated Him enough to kill Him — which they did. When Jesus claimed to be the "I Am," eternally existent long before Abraham (v 58), they attempted to stone Him. But He refused to die this way. He had a date with a wooden cross on which He would give Himself as the sacrifice for their sins and ours only a few days later. They killed

73

Him because of His claim to be God (Mark 14:53-65).

Jesus Christ was not simply a great moral teacher. Either He was a liar, He was out of His mind, or He was God in human flesh as He claimed. If He lied and knew He was lying, He was also a fool because He gave His life for what He declared. If He didn't know He was lying, He was a deluded lunatic. But Someone who lived as He lived and taught as He taught could not have been out of His mind. The only alternative any rational person can conclude is that Jesus Christ is exactly who He claimed to be — the LORD of Glory!

Our judgment is limited because we don't know all the facts. We must either accept the speculation of men or the revelation of God. God has revealed Himself in Jesus Christ, His One and Only Son. What do you believe about Him? You must decide what to believe. But remember, what you decide doesn't change the fact of who He is — the eternally existent Son of the Living God. It simply changes your eternal destiny!

Read 1 Corinthians 15

For what I received I passed on to you as of first importance:
that Christ died for our sins according to the Scriptures, that he
was buried, that he was raised on the third day according to
the Scriptures, and that he appeared to Peter, and then to the
Twelve. After that, he appeared to more than five hundred of
the brothers at the same time, most of whom are still living,
though some have fallen asleep.

1 Corinthians 15:3-6

Seventh inning —
THE MOST IMPORTANT THING

IN BASEBALL, the most important part of the game is
pitching. Some managers feel it is 70 percent of the
game. Others feel it may be as much as 80 or 85 percent
of the game. If a team has a dominant pitcher on the
mound, their chances of victory are excellent, for a rule
of thumb is "good pitching, beats good hitting."

In 1 Corinthians 15:3-6, Paul tells us what is of first
importance in the game of life. This passage is an answer to the first heresy of the early church. That heresy
was the denial of the bodily resurrection of Jesus Christ.
Though it is still around today, one cannot really be a
Christian and deny the death, burial, and resurrection
of Jesus Christ.

It is because of His resurrection that we have any
hope at all. Because He rose from the dead, it is con-
firmed who He was: the only begotten Son of God. Because He is God, He cannot lie. Therefore, all He said
about coming back to take those who believe in Him to
live in heaven with Him will take place! Sin, Satan, and
death are defeated. We win, because he arose from the
dead!

Jesus arose bodily. It was a physical resurrection.
The word is *anastasis nekion*, which means "the standing up of a corpse." There is no gospel ("good news")
without the resurrection of Jesus Christ. It is the basis

of our faith. The very foundation of Christianity is the fact of the resurrection. The tomb was empty. All the unbelieving Jewish religious leaders had to do to forever destroy Christianity was to produce His body. But He arose and was seen by hundreds of people who were still alive to verify the fact (v 6). Because of this fact, many believed upon Him. Through nineteen centuries, millions of people have believed Jesus Christ arose from the dead.

The scattered, fearful disciples had their lives transformed by the fact of Christ's resurrection. They laid down their lives for Him. Many (soldiers in Nazi Germany) have died for a lie, but they *thought* it was the truth. But men do not die for what they *know* to be a lie. The disciples were convinced Jesus was alive when they saw and touched Him!

This life is not all there is. Because of the resurrection of Jesus Christ, we know there is another life to follow. What an implication for our lifestyles! What hope we have for the future!

Read 2 Corinthians 5:1-10

So we make it our goal to please Him, whether we are at home in the body or away from it. For we must all appear before the judgment seat of Christ, that each one may receive what is due him for the things done while in the body, whether good or bad.
1 Corinthians 5:9, 10

Seventh inning —
JESUS' BOX SEAT

DURING THE HEIGHT of their empire, the Greeks placed a high premium on winning in athletic competitions. While the losers were virtually ignored, the winners were escorted before a box seat called the "bema". There sat the commissioner of the games. As the winner approached, he was presented a victory wreath in a glamorous and noble ceremony.

While unbelievers are destined to be judged at the Great White Throne (Revelation 20:11-15), all those who are saved by God's grace will one day stand before the "bema" of the Lord Jesus Christ. This judgment is not to determine whether Christians will be saved in Heaven or lost in hell, for the salvation of all who trust Christ is already guaranteed (John 6:37-40, 10:28). This "ceremony" is for the purpose of awarding or denying "crowns" to Christians for faithfulness to God in this life! Such a judgment is alarming enough to the child of God! Every opportunity God has given us to glorify Him in thought, word, and deed will be considered. And God is very impartial. He knows what time, talent, and treasure He has given us in this life. He knows the motive behind every action we have taken! And He will reward accordingly (1 Corinthians 4:4, 5).

We must be "wise builders" in this life, for the Lord will test our works with fire (1 Corinthians 3:10-15). How tragic to lose the rewards we might have enjoyed had we lived entirely for Him! How wonderful to be rewarded with one of the five crowns mentioned in

Scripture! There is the Imperishable Crown (1 Corinthians 9:24-27) given for self discipline; the Crown of Rejoicing (1 Thessalonians 2:19) given for sowing good seed in the lives of others; the Crown of Life (James 1:12; Revelation 2:10) given for enduring trials for Christ's sake; the Crown of Righteousness (2 Timothy 4:8) given for living in purity while looking forward to His coming again; and the Crown of Glory (1 Peter 5:4) given for leadership of God's people.

Can you visualize standing before the "box seat" of Jesus Christ, the Commissioner of the Game of Life? What prizes will He be able to present to you? If you spend your life giving, loving, and serving Him by the power of His Spirit, your rewards will be great.

Eighth inning —

THE CHURCH

The Real One . . .

JESUS CHRIST

Inning	1	2	3	4	5	6	7	8	9	10
SATAN	0	Fall	0	0	Slavery	Captivity	Crucifixion	Suffering		
GOD	Creation	Promise	Flood	Abraham	Israel	David	Resurrection	Spirit		

How They Scored

Eighth inning —
God sent the Holy Spirit as promised . . . the believers in Jesus receive His power . . . they go everywhere on earth telling of His resurrection and promise of life to all who turn from sin to Him . . . the church is inconsistent down through the years . . . Satan hounds it at every turn . . . persecutions help keep it strong.

79

Read Acts 2

When the day of Pentecost came, they were all together in one place. Suddenly a sound like the blowing of a violent wind came from heaven and filled the whole house where they were sitting. They saw what seemed to be tongues of fire that separated and came to rest on each of them. All of them were filled with the Holy Spirit and began to speak in other tongues (languages) as the Spirit enabled them.

Acts 2:1-4

Eighth inning —

POWERIZED

THE HILLERICH AND BRADSBY COMPANY has stamped the word "Powerized" on their Louisville Slugger bats for decades. It's a promotion to signify the quality inside the bat. Certainly, in the hands of stars like Jose Canseco, Ken Griffey Jr., and Cecil Fielder, a Louisville Slugger is powerized!

Christians become "powerized" when the Holy Spirit comes to indwell them. This first happened on the day of Pentecost. Jesus Christ had been raised from the dead and returned to Heaven. At one point, He had told His followers to wait in Jerusalem until the next event on His agenda (Acts 1). That event was the sending of the powerful Holy Spirit of God, which would signal the beginning of the "church" age. With the coming of the Holy Spirit, Christians would have power to live and to communicate the reality of a living Christ.

Acts 2 describes the coming of this wonderful Third Person of the Trinity. Pentecost, a feast day for Israel, was chosen by God as the day He sent His Spirit to indwell those who believed in His Son. His presence was indicated in two ways: the *sound* of a violent wind and the *sight* of flames of fire! And the presence of the Holy Spirit in the lives of believers changed *everything!* Now they had power when telling others of the resurrection of Jesus Christ! Peter immediately preached a sermon

(Acts 2) and three thousand people put their faith in Christ and were baptized! Every other sermon that the disciples preached was on the resurrection of Jesus — with dramatic results!

The Holy Spirit is the Christian life. No man has power to live for Christ apart from His power. He remains active today in the lives of all who belong to Jesus. He is our power! He is our life!

Read Acts 9

But the Lord said to Ananias, "Go! This man (Paul) is my chosen instrument to carry my name before the Gentiles and their kings and before the people of Israel. I will show him how much he must suffer for my name."

Acts 9:15, 16

Eighth inning —
PAUL: ALL-STAR APOSTLE

EVERY JULY, the Major League All-star game features baseball's best players. And every all-star game has an MVP. In 1994, Fred McGriff of the Braves was chosen. McGriff hit a 2-run home run in the ninth inning to send the game into extra innings. When the National League won in extra innings, his homer was recognized as the crucial turning point.

Saul was a highly educated Pharisee. He was a leader of the religious Jews who hated the fact that Jesus Christ had been raised from the dead and that thousands were now following Him. He hated the Christians enough to kill them. In fact, he was in the process of doing exactly that when the risen Christ appeared to him!

Saul was radically changed. He became known as Paul, the greatest apostle in church history. Certainly, he was one of Jesus' MVPs! But Paul didn't become a great servant of the Lord Jesus without suffering. Suffering for Christ was his constant companion. Suffering became God's means of making Paul humble. Because Paul was shown his own limits and accepted them, God gave him great grace and fruit in his labor. Listen to his story:

"But we have this treasure in jars of clay to show that this all-surpassing power is from God and not from us. We are hard pressed on every side, but not crushed; perplexed, but not in despair; persecuted, but not abandoned; struck down, but not destroyed" (1 Corinthians 4:7-9).

83

Paul suffered much trouble in beatings, stonings, imprisonments, shipwrecks, hard work, sleepless nights, hunger and slander from others (2 Corinthians 6:3-10, 11:23-33). He was given a "thorn in the flesh" to keep him from becoming conceited (2 Corinthians 12:7). But God promised to give Paul grace to overcome anything (v 9). The "all-star apostle" realized that the power of Christ rested upon him in his weakness, so he delighted in his weaknesses. He was strong in Christ when weak in himself (v 10).

The Apostle Paul took the gospel to the Gentile world. He wrote much of the New Testament. His life and influence continues today because of his sufferings for Christ in the early days of the church. What an eternal investment was made by one of Jesus' "star" players!

Yet, I hold this against you: You have left your first love.

Revelation 2:4

Eighth inning —
Ephesus: Inconsistent Christians

THE DIFFERENCE between a major league ball player and a minor leaguer may not be in physical strength or even in skill. Consistency is the key. A major league player must make plays over and over with a minimum of mistakes. When the ball is hit to him, he performs consistently. Otherwise, he'll soon find himself back in the minors!

Since Jesus Christ returned to Heaven, His visible "body" on earth has been the church. But the church has been an imperfect, inconsistent example of His nature. The church has deserved to be sent back to the minor leagues! In Revelation 2 and 3, Jesus gave seven messages to the pastors ("angels" or "messengers") of churches in Asia Minor. These types of people and churches exist today, and will exist until His return. In addition, these churches represent seven periods of history through which the Church of Christ has passed. Though He commended many traits in the churches, He also had words of warning.

Ephesus, where John (the writer) had lived for about 30 years, was the religious and commercial center of influence over Europe as well as over Asia. It was a city filled with materialism, basc idol worship, and darkness. Jesus had a word for the church in that city. He speaks not to the lost people in his message, for it is futile to ask an unsaved person to do good deeds. But after a person accepts Christ and is saved, Jesus has much to say about doing good works. The Ephesian church was a hard working, suffering church which would not tolerate the high and mighty clergymen (Nicolatians) who presented themselves as "super spiritual" over the common man. Jesus commended this attitude, but pointed out that despite their hard work and perseverance they had lost their first love — the intense love for Jesus Himself! Without great love of the Savior, they really would have no influence for Him. Because their light had failed, unless they would repent He would have to remove their "lampstand" (influence).

Christians first get sidetracked not by gross sins, great doctrinal error, or by Satanic attack. Losing ground in our lives begins when we lose the intense, "first love" for Jesus Christ Himself. We forget how wonderful He is to us. We lose sight of the blood He shed to pay for our sins and guarantee us Heaven instead of Hell. We become cold, then skeptical, cynical and indifferent. Materialism begins to steal our enthusiasm for Christ.

What is your feeling for Christ today? Is it red hot in love with the One who took your lashes on His back, had a crown of thorns pressed into His head, and was nailed to the cross you deserved? Or have you forgotten where you came from and become cold and inconsistent toward Him? Remember and repent and your love will again become "hot."

Read Revelation 2:8-11

I know your afflictions and your poverty — yet you are rich! I know the slander of those who say they are Jews and are not, but are a synagogue of Satan. Do not be afraid of what you are about to suffer. I tell you, the devil will put some of you in prison to test you, and you will suffer persecution for ten days. Be faithful, even to the point of death, and I will give you the crown of life.

Revelation 2:9, 10

Eighth inning —
SMYRNA: SUFFERING CHRISTIANS

FORMER RED SOX first baseman Billy Buckner suffered much as he recalled the weak ground ball that went between his legs in Game 6 of the 1986 World Series. The ninth-inning error allowed the New York Mets to stay alive and to win the series in Game 7. Billy was hounded by people and personal memories since that day. Finally, he sold his World Series ring for $33,000 and wrote a personal note of authenticity. "Hope you enjoy my 1986 World Series ring," he said. "The nightmare of 1986 is over. I'm off the hook."

Bill Buckner's suffering is minuscule compared to the suffering of Christians during the Roman persecutions. Imperial laws against Christianity were severely enforced in the wicked city of Smyrna. From 100 AD (the period of time represented by the Smyrna Church) bloody persecution of believers was carried out by the Roman Empire. *Foxes' Book of Martyrs* reports that five million Christians were killed during this period. Jesus had not one word of criticism for the church at Smyrna. *He knew all about their poverty and their suffering.* It was a long time before their "nightmare" was over.

Yet, the Christian never really loses when he suffers and dies for Christ. Paul said, "To live is Christ, and to die is gain" (Philippians 1:21). Christians are victorious over death because we identify with Jesus' victory over

87

death and the grave. We overcome by His blood and our testimony (Revelation 12:11). Faith is the victory that overcomes the world (1 John 5:4).

Why do Christians suffer? Sometimes we do not know. But our faith gets strongest when we keep on believing in spite of what we see. Sometimes we suffer as discipline from God for unconfessed sin (1 Corinthians 11:30). Sometimes God permits a messenger of Satan (sickness or injury) to prevent inflated egos (2 Corinthians 12:7). Sometimes we suffer to learn obedience (Hebrews 5:8). Sometimes we suffer simply because we live in a sinful world which hates our Jesus (Acts 9:16). Sometimes God allows suffering to display His work in us (John 9:2, 3). We also suffer to enable us to empathize with others who suffer (2 Corinthians 1:3-7). Who can comfort people like those who have suffered similarly? Sometimes we suffer to produce growth in character (Romans 5:3-5). Some Christians suffer to advance the gospel (Philippians 1:12-14).

Suffering helps us to place our hopes in God and not in ourselves (2 Corinthians 1:8-11). Whether you know why you are suffering or not, place your hope in the One who will never forsake you. God has promised to stay with us (Hebrews 13:5). He is the trustworthy One in all our suffering.

Read Revelation 2:12-17

I know where you live — where Satan has his throne. Yet you remain true to my name. You did not renounce your faith in me, even in the days of Antipas, my faithful witness, who was put to death in your city — where Satan lives. Nevertheless, I have a few things against you . . .

Revelation 2:13, 14

Eighth inning —

PERGAMUM:
COMFORTABLE WITH THE ENEMY

ARGENTINE SOCCER STAR Diego Maradona just couldn't keep from compromising with his own worst enemy — banned drugs. In 1994, at the age of 33, the brilliant Maradona was steering his country toward the final of the World Cup for the third time. But he robbed himself of one last chance to shed his outlaw reputation by testing positive for five banned substances. He was suspended from the World Cup on June 29, and his team fell to Bulgaria the next day in what would have been his record-setting 22nd World Cup match. His compromise with drugs had led to his downfall.

Ephesus and Smyrna were evil cities, but Pergamum was worse! The church in Pergamum had so compromised itself with the evil world around her that it became comfortable with sin. She was elevated in power and became socially acceptable, but lost power with God in the process. Satan himself had moved his earthly headquarters to Pergamum. Through the "teaching of Balaam," who taught foreign nations to lure God's people away from Jehovah, the church at Pergamum had allied itself with the world. There is *no power* from God when we compromise with the world.

Jesus knew all about the tough circumstances under which the Pergamum church existed. He knew it lived in Satan's headquarters (v 13), the religious city of

89

Pergamum. Bible scholars believe he had been head-quartered in Babylon, moved to Pergamum, and later to Rome (McGee believed he now works out of Los Angeles!). The LORD commends the church at Pergamum for holding to his name in spite of adverse outward circumstances. But now that Satan has failed to destroy the church from the outside, he moves *inside* to destroy it. Jesus condemns the toleration of Balaam's doctrine (idolatry and sexual looseness) in the church. He called the church to repent of tolerating the teaching of the Nicolaitans: Moral laxity and religious rituals which ignored the priesthood of *all* believers. The Word of God, not the church, is the only authority for deciding right and wrong!

As Jesus said to his people in Pergamum, "I know where you live (v 13), He knows where you and I live, also. He knows our circumstances. He knows about Satanic attacks against us, for Satan is not in Hell (yet). He is a religious person and when he can't *beat* us, he *joins* us for church! He tries to replace our relationship (to Christ) with religion and with religious thoughts and deeds. When the approval of the world replaces our walk with Jesus, we exchange a life of victory for mere formal outward appearance. What a bad deal! Let's not make it!

Read Revelation 2:18-29

Nevertheless, I have this against you: You tolerate that woman Jezebel, who calls herself a prophetess. By her teaching she misleads my servants into sexual immorality and the eating of food sacrificed to idols.

Revelation 2:20

Eighth inning —
THYATIRA: MOVING FAST IN THE WRONG DIRECTION

THE NAME ROY RIEGALS has become synonomous with "wrong direction." As a California linebacker in the 1929 Rose Bowl, Roy scooped up a Georgia Tech fumble, got turned around, and raced 75 yards in the wrong direction. Teammate Benny Lom finally caught him at his own one-yard line. Cal tried to punt the ball out of their own end zone on the next play, but the kick was blocked and Tech scored an 8-7 victory!

Riegals' story doesn't end with a wrong run, however. He returned for the second half and played a most outstanding game. The next year, Roy was elected Captain and even gained mention as an All-American. Later in life, Roy Riegals became a successful coach and businessman. He recovered from great humiliation to achieve great success.

The church at Thyatira was an example of a whole group of people who worked hard but were running in the wrong direction. Jesus wrote his longest, most severe letter to this very active group who loved him and had faith, but was becoming morally corrupt. Thyatira (which means "continual sacrifice") represents those who think they have to offer continual penance to appease God, instead of trusting in the finished work of Christ on the cross to pay for sins.

Whenever a woman is used symbolically in Scripture, she represents false religion. Jezebel, an adulterous Old

Testament ruler who persecuted Israel, is descriptive of the church in Thyatira and of many churches today. She represents compromise with the world, false religion, empty profession, dead formalism, doctrinal perversion, and paganism within the church. Included in this "religious mess" is the belief in one man (pope) as "vicar" of Christ on earth. Also included is worship of Mary or any of the saints, toleration of adultery and homosexuality, and religious rituals that are not taught in God's Word. We have a "baptized paganism" in many churches today. Many have turned Christianity into a religion instead of a relationship. Jesus has been made to take a secondary role. No pope, preacher, priest, pastor, or any other religious dictator can take Jesus' place. He is "Numero Uno!" He will judge the living and the dead. No church is God's authority on earth. The Holy Spirit, resident in each true believer, is God's authority. God's "vicar" on earth is not a man — He is the Spirit of the living God!

Are you working hard at your religion, but running in the wrong direction? Return to the Word of God for guidance. Seek His teaching and not that of any church or man. Men and organizations can be wrong, but God's Word, taught by God's Spirit to your heart, never fails to lead you in the right direction. He will restore you and help you to run successfully. Rest in Him for help and guidance.

Read Revelation 3:1-6

I know your deeds; you have a reputation of being alive, but you are dead.

Revelation 3:1

Eighth inning —
SARDIS: DEAD AS A DOORNAIL

MANY TIMES THE NEWS MEDIA can make or break a reputation or an athlete's career. The public makes conclusions based upon what is printed or neglected to be printed. This is unfortunate, but it means we must be careful to distinguish between character and reputation. A reputation is what other people *think* we are, while character is what we *really* are when no one else is looking.

The church at Sardis had a reputation for being alive, but was quite dead. This church represents Protestantism, with its divisions and deadness. While the Catholic Church (Thyatira) was corrupt and pagan, great reformers like Martin Luther, John Huss, and John Wesley led a Reformation. Some (not all) of the truths of Scripture were re-discovered. But the reformers died, and the movement faded into systems, dogma and the traditions of men. Worse yet, the Protestant churches became state churches across Europe, embracing the entire population and minimizing a personal relationship with Jesus Christ. The reputation (what others think you are) of being alive was tempered by the reality of dead formalism.

Today, many dead denominations deny the cardinal truths of Christianity. Some have embraced the World Council of Churches, which tries to unite all churches into one false religious system. These churches have a religious *profession* without *possession* of genuine faith. Tim LaHaye says, "If people leave church with a mysterious 'feeling of worship' but have not been brought face

93

to face with Jesus Christ in a personal way, they have been worshiping in a dead church."

Jesus warned us to wake up in expectation of His coming! There is no deadness in a church, or an individual that is eagerly anticipating the return of Christ!

All believers are "overcomers" (1 John 4:4; Romans 8:31-39). Like the home team in an athletic contest, overcomers will wear white when He comes to take us home! The character (what we really are) of a real Christian matches his reputation. A real believer may attend a dead church, but he is alive on the inside! As Jesus implied (Matthew 7:13, 14), true believers may be few, but God always has a remnant.

How about you? Are you alive on the inside, or do you only profess to be alive? Do you have the constant joy of the Holy Spirit as you wait, watch and pray for Christ's return? Does your character *really* match your reputation? If so, praise God! If not, why not exchange the dead formalism of your religion for new life in Jesus Christ?

Read Revelation 3:7-13

I am coming soon. Hold on to what you have so that no one will take your crown.

Revelation 3:11

Eighth inning —
PHILADELPHIA: HOLD ON TO JESUS

IT TOOK A WHOLE SEASON for the 1906 Montreal Wanderers to win the Stanley Cup. Yet it took only a few hours to lose hockey's most coveted prize. The team left the trophy at a drunken celebration. The next day, a cleaning lady found the abandoned silver cup, took it home, and used it as a flowerpot for geraniums!

The city of Philadelphia (which means "brotherly love") was named after Attatus Philadelphus, king of Pergamum (159-138 BC), because of his loyalty to his brother Eumenes. Though the church in Philadelphia was weak, her future was bright because the believers had obeyed God's Word and had not denied His Name in spite of adversity. Jesus had no condemnation for her! This church is a picture of true Christians just before Jesus returns to rapture ("catch away") them to Heaven. He promises to save us from the hour of trial (the Great Tribulation) that is coming upon the whole world (v 10)!

Jesus said He would come "soon" (v 11). The idea is that He will come "suddenly" or "quickly." The doctrine of the imminence of Christ's return motivates us to serve Him. Unlike the 1906 Montreal Wanderers, we must hold on to Him by faith so we will not lose rewards for deeds done in His service. Our *salvation* cannot be lost (He paid for and secured it), but our *rewards* (crowns) are another issue. Words and deeds done for Jesus will be rewarded, but selfish, lazy living resulting in lost opportunities will end in loss of rewards from our Master. How sad to lose what we might have earned! We *must* serve Him!

95

It is Jesus who holds the "key of David" (Revelation 3:7). He will reign on the earth. He also holds the key of death and hell (Revelation 1:18). He controls death and the grave and will release all those who have trusted Him! It is Jesus who opens the doors of opportunity to serve Him where He leads, but we cannot kick open any door He has closed! Jesus must provide the coaching position, teaching job, business opening, administrative role, or whatever job you are to fulfill for His glory (2 Corinthians 2:12). Let us follow His leading and serve Him and others with the "brotherly love" of the Philadelphia church.

Read Revelation 3:14-22

I know your deeds, that you are neither cold nor hot; I wish you were either one or the other! So, because you are lukewarm — neither hot nor cold — I am about to spit you out of my mouth.

Revelation 3:15, 16

Eighth inning —

LAODICEA: LUKEWARMNESS

OREL HERSHISER was an inconsistent rookie trying to stay in the big leagues in 1984. He was up and down, too passive to really get the job done. His manager, Tommy Lasorda, was loud and assertive. No one doubted where he stood. One day, Lasorda called Herschiser into the office for a tongue-lashing.
"You don't believe in yourself!" Tommy said. "You're scared to pitch in the big leagues! Who do you think these hitters are, Babe Ruth? Ruth's dead! You've got good stuff. If you didn't, I wouldn't have brought you up. Quit bein' so careful! Go after the hitters! " Lasorda then nicknamed him "Bulldog" with the challenge to live up to the name. The session worked. Hershiser's career was turned around. Instead of lukewarm performances, he became red hot!

Laodicea was a wealthy Greek city of commerce. There was so much wealth that when an earthquake destroyed the city 35 years prior to the letter John wrote to the church there, the city leaders rejected Rome's help and rebuilt themselves! The church in Laodicea reflected the culture more than reflecting Jesus. It was self-sufficient, indifferent to Jesus, and felt it had no needs. Their lukewarm attitude of indifference was the most dangerous of all the churches. If the church had been cold it might have seen a need and repented. If it had been hot, Jesus would have commended it. But the dull, bland indifference of lukewarmness was nauseous to a holy God, who promised to "spit it out" faster than Tommy Lasorda would have demoted Orel Hershiser.

They had a profession of faith and carried on business as usual, but had no love for Jesus. It was in the church "business," with organization, programs, and committees. But though it made a claim on Christ, He didn't claim them! Blind to its poverty of spirit, this church had no power with God.

Though God loves rich people, in most cases material riches are not conducive to spiritual vitality. While the Philadelphia church would be "caught up" to be with Jesus, the Laodicean church would be "spit out." Jesus counsel is to repent of lukewarmness and "get hot" (zealous) for God. He stands outside the door of His own modern church knocking for permission to enter! He has all authority in heaven and on earth, but He won't force that authority on anyone today. That day will come during the millennium. He has already moved heaven and earth to save mankind, but if the organized church will not let Him rule, He will turn and let it self-destruct. His authority and even His influence is waning in many churches. Someone else (a majority vote, a hierarchy of leaders) is making decisions in His place.

How about you personally? Jesus still knocks on the "heart's door" of individuals. Is He a figurehead you say you serve while you really run your own life? Are you indifferent to His knock? You have no guarantee He will knock indefinitely. Life is short. Talk is cheap. It's repentance He is seeking.

Ninth inning —

THE SECOND
COMING OF CHRIST

A STUDY OF 1 AND 2 THESSALONIANS

The Real One . . .

JESUS CHRIST

Inning	1	2	3	4	5	6	7	8	9	10
SATAN	0	Fall	0	0	Slavery	Captivity	Crucifixion	Suffering	Deception	
GOD	Creation	Promise	Flood	Abraham	Israel	David	Resurrection	Spirit	Rapture	

How They Scored

Ninth inning —

Adversities for Christians grow worse and worse . . . God's people are refined. . . suddenly they are snatched away to meet Jesus in the air . . . A great leader claiming to be god unites the world economically, militarily, and religiously . . . peace and protection is promised as this dictator rules the world.

Introduction
First Thessalonians

THESSALONICA was a strategic city of 200,000 people. On his second mission, the Apostle Paul visited this city for approximately three weeks, teaching the people about Jesus and the truths of Christianity. So many Jewish people (and Gentiles) believed his message, the membership in the synagogue was depleted and irate Jews ran Paul out of town! It seems that everywhere Paul preached about Jesus, either a riot or a revival (sometimes both) resulted!

Later, Paul became concerned for the new Christians in the city. While in Corinth between 50 AD and 52 AD, he wrote his first letter to them. He wrote to a model church (1:7) which thrived despite strong opposition (1:6, 2:14). Paul had not gone to Thessalonica for any selfish reason, for he gained nothing but persecution by going there. He wrote out of a warm heart to answer questions and to instruct. His instruction especially concerned the second coming of Christ to remove His people from the world. Paul writes about our attitude toward Christ's return (ch. 1), our reward at His return (ch. 2), our life until His return (ch. 3-4:12), our death if it is prior to His return (4:13-18), and our actions in light of His return (ch. 5). In Chapter Five he gives 22 commands in view of Christ's return for His people.

As you study this letter, may God cause you to become a model of His grace and peace! And as you await Christ's return, may He infuse you with the joy of knowing He is coming for you!

Read 1 Thessalonians 1:1-3

We continually remember before our God and Father your work produced by faith, your labor prompted by love, and your endurance inspired by hope in our Lord Jesus Christ.

1 Thessalonians 1:3

Ninth inning —
POSITIVE ROLE MODELS

MANY ATHLETES, former athletes, and coaches are positive role models for youth in our society. But others feel no responsibility when it comes to their lifestyles, living for self and, like Charles Barkley, denying that they are emulated by others. Our sports pages are littered with accounts of substance abuse, divorce, and even murder charges against some of our most visible athletic heroes.

The new Christians in Thessalonica were dramatically changed by their belief in Jesus. Paul said they were a model to other believers (v 7). In following Paul's example and the example of the Lord, they became role models! How we need more positive role models in our society today!

What traits did the Thessalonians model? In the *past,* they had put their faith in God, which resulted in good works. If we really have faith in God, our lives will be transformed. True faith works in more ways than one! Theirs was not a syrupy, sentimental faith, but a practical, working faith in God.

At *present,* their motivation was love in the service of the true and living God (v 9). It's easy to work for someone you love. A little girl was carrying a heavy baby. A man passing by said to her, "Isn't that baby too heavy for you?" She answered, "He isn't heavy. He's my brother." Love isn't labor when it's a labor of love.

For the *future,* we have the great hope of our Lord's return! Therefore, we wait with patient endurance.

Martin Luther said, "Everything that is done in the world is done by hope." O. S. Marden says, "There is no medicine like hope, no incentive so great, and no tonic so powerful as expectation of something better tomorrow." Our hope is not in man, or in the world, or in a political party, or in hope itself. Our sure hope is in Jesus! J. Vernon McGee said, "The scepter of this universe is in nail-pierced hands, and He will move at the right time."

Despite severe persecution, the Thessalonian believers remained true role models. They provided an example. What kind of example are you setting? If it is a model of faith, love, and hope, others can safely follow.

Read 1 Thessalonians 1:4-10

. . . you turned to God from idols to serve the living and true God, and to wait for his son from heaven, whom he raised from the dead — Jesus, who rescues us from the coming wrath.
1 Thessalonians 1:9, 10

Ninth inning —
PICKED OFF THE PLANET

A WELL-TIMED PICKOFF play has gotten many a pitcher out of a severe jam when things seemed the worst. Pickoffs have completely changed the momentum of a baseball game. For this reason, coaches spend much time drilling pitchers on pickoffs.

Infielder Gary Gaetti was dramatically changed when he met Jesus in the 1980s. Now he looks forward to another kind of pickoff. "I've got to play baseball," he said. "It's my job. We're supposed to work. I can't scream and shout at the other team like I used to. But in ways I lead — I just do it a little different . . . But to tell you the truth; I wish Jesus would come back now and let us all go to heaven. This world doesn't compare to what heaven is like." Gary is waiting for Jesus to " pick us off" this earth!

As stated earlier, the Christians at Thessalonica were a model to believers in other cities. Chosen ("selected") by God (v 4), they had turned to Him from idols and were now actively waiting for Jesus to "pick them off" the earth and save them from the wrath of God.

The Thessalonians knew they were chosen by God (v 4). How can we understand God's election of lost sinners and man's responsibility to trust Him? With our finite minds, we can't. No one has ever explained it adequately. But the Bible teaches both as true. Just as our ears cannot hear some high pitched sounds, our minds cannot comprehend some truths of God.

The Thessalonian Christians had turned from idols

because they had turned to God (v 9). One automatically follows the other. To illustrate: If you are in Nashville and want to go to Atlanta, you automatically leave Nashville. When a person worships idols and turns to God (believes), he automatically turns away from (repents) idols in this world. The two go together.

Now, the Thessalonians were waiting to be rescued by the return of Jesus. Every chapter in this letter closes with a reference to His return. It is a fact that God's wrath will be poured out on an unbelieving world. Christians are objects of His mercy, not of His wrath (Romans 9:22, 23). He has not appointed us to suffer His wrath, but to be saved (1 Thessalonians 5:9). The wrath of God is being revealed against all the godlessness and wickedness of men who suppress the truth (Romans 1:8). The wrath of God remains upon all who reject Jesus (John 3:36). One day, during the Great Tribulation, God will pour out His wrath on all unbelievers. Mighty men will call on rocks and mountains to fall on them to hide them from His terrible wrath (Revelation 6:15-17). One day, Jesus will execute God's wrath against unrepentant sinners (Revelation 19:11-16). But Paul tells us that Jesus will rescue His believers from God's wrath. He is coming from Heaven to "catch us up" for a meeting with Him in the air and to keep us with Him forever (4:17)! That is the "pickoff" we await! Jesus will save us from God's wrath. What a great <u>save</u> that will be!

Read 1 Thessalonians 2:1-20

For what is our hope, our joy, or the crown in which we will glory in the presence of our Lord Jesus when He comes? Is it not you?

1 Thessalonians 2:19

Ninth inning —
THE CROWN IN WHICH WE GLORY

SOCCER TEAMS gathered in America from all over the world during the summer of 1994. They competed in pursuit of an award called the "World Cup." Winning the World Cup Games has become a national passion in many countries, and small wars have broken out because of this passion. Many nations see great glory in competing for this piece of metal!

Christians glory in rewards much different from soccer's World Cup. Paul was an example. He had suffered insult, beating, and imprisonment in Phillipi. Yet, it had not changed his boldness in sharing with people the way of salvation. He spoke from pure motives. He was not trying to build a reputation as a great preacher. He did not try to trick or to flatter those who listened. He supported himself, so as not to burden anyone financially.

Despite many who believed the gospel, many other Jews in Thessalonica refused to believe. They persecuted those who trusted Jesus and they drove Paul out of town (v 15). As Paul wrote to the believers in Thessalonica, he revealed his deep feelings for them. Knowing of their sincere commitment to Christ, he loved them deeply. He called them his hope, his joy, and the crown in which he would glory when Jesus returned.

It is an established fact that Jesus is coming — first *for* His church (the rapture) and (seven years later) *with* His church (the revelation) to reign on the earth. After He comes for His people, He will reward them based upon their faithfulness and obedience to His will. As

Paul followed God's direction to Thessalonica, many were "born again" into the family of God. Paul called these people His "crown." The word he chose was used for a wreath awarded to the winners of athletic games or to distinguish public officials of his day. In 2 Corinthians 5:10, Paul said we (believers) must all stand before the judgment seat ("bema") of Christ to be rewarded according to our faithfulness. Note that we are not being assigned to heaven or to hell at this judgment, but we are to receive or be denied rewards. The "bema" was the "box seat" where the judge of the ancient athletic contests sat and from which he gave out rewards (wreaths) to the winners. Paul called the Thessalonian Christians the "crown" in which he would find glory when Jesus returned. What a thrill he had and would later have because of these dear people!

In what or in whom do you find hope and joy? Where will your crown of glory be when Jesus returns? Are there others whom you have influenced for Christ who will be with Jesus because of your faithfulness and obedience to Him? If so, you may glory in His rewards at His return! The World Cup will seem very insignificant on that day.

Read 1 Thessalonians 3:1-13

. . . so that no one would be unsettled by these trials. You know quite well that we were destined for them.

1 Thessalonians 3:3

Ninth inning —
DESTINED FOR TRIALS

DETROIT TIGER OUTFIELDER Kirk Gibson knows how to live with pain. In 1980, he tore cartilage in his wrist. In 1982, he had a sore left knee, a strained calf muscle, and a severe wrist sprain. A year later, he was out for knee surgery. In 1985, he was hit in the mouth with a pitch and required 17 stitches. He also bruised a hamstring, injured his right heel, and had a sore left ankle. In 1986, Kirk severely injured a ligament in his ankle. Concerning pain, Kirk was quoted as saying, "There are pluses and minuses in everything we do in life . . . But the pluses for my career, myself, and my family make it worth it. It's the path I chose."

When we chose to follow Christ, we also chose a path of pain. Therefore, Christians should not be surprised by trials. That's the message of Paul to the Thessalonian believers who suffered (v 4). Fanatical religious people (Jews) who had created God in their own image persecuted believers in the Jewish Messiah. Craftsmen who earned much money from making and selling idols harassed Christians because faith in a living Savior hurt their businesses. Multitudes who knew nothing about God, His love, and His eagerness to forgive were irritated by this strange new group which made them uncomfortable in their sin.

Paul was concerned that the Christians would be "unsettled." Literally, he was afraid they would "waver back and forth like the tail of a wagging dog" in their trials. He needn't have worried. After visiting the city, Timothy returned to Paul and reported the strength of the Thessalonian's faith and love. This report brought Paul much joy.

We must expect trials in this world. Jesus promised they would come (John 16:13). Paul said that all who live godly lives will suffer (2 Timothy 3:12). But trials are not our enemies (James 1:2-4)! Rather than becoming "unsettled" by returning to a worldly lifestyle, denying Christ, or yielding to temptation, may we allow trials to develop perseverance, character, and hope (Romans 5:3-5). And Godly hope will never disappoint us!

Read 1 Thessalonians 4:1-10

Finally, brothers, we instructed you how to live in order to please God, as in fact you are living.

1 Thessalonians 4:1

Ninth inning —
OUR GOAL WHILE WE WAIT

RESEARCH SHOWS that goal-setting gives many people much better focus and direction. There is truth in the statement, "aim at nothing and you'll hit it every time!" Paul was glad to know the Thessalonians were pursuing the goal of pleasing God. He encouraged them to do so more and more.

"Coach" Paul gave instructions on how to reach the goal of pleasing God. First, he wrote that we should be "sanctified." To be sanctified means to be "set apart" in thought, word, and deed from the evil around us. It means to be "holy," becoming more dedicated to God every day. Sanctification relates to our bodies. In Greek culture, temple prostitutes ensnared worshipers in sexual sins which became a popular part of worship. Few spoke out against such heathen behavior as multitudes degraded themselves via loose sexual behavior. Paul wrote that Christians must not wrong ("defraud") other brothers by such immorality. When we engage in any sex outside of marriage, we have cheated the other person, robbed him/her of honor, and violated the laws of love. There are dire consequences for such sin, ranging far beyond unwanted pregnancy, AIDS, or other sexually transmitted diseases. A grieved and callous spirit, the loss of innocence and self-respect, and a division of spirit result from our lack of self-control. We must control (rule) the temple (body) of God's Spirit (1 Corinthians 6:19).

Secondly, we are to love our brothers in Christ. Christians are to love everyone, but we have a special

111

love for other believers. God teaches us intuitively to love our brothers (v 9). In loving them, we will seek their good fortune.

Finally, Christians are to win the respect of unbelievers and not be dependent upon others for financial help. We do so by working hard in all we do. While the Greeks detested manual labor and used slaves as much as possible, the Jews taught each young boy a trade by which to support himself. Jesus was a carpenter and Paul a tentmaker. The apostles all had a profession or trade.

As we await the return of Jesus Christ, we must not wait passively. We have a goal to please God, and we please Him when we control our bodies, love others, and win the respect of outsiders by our hard work. Becoming goal-oriented to please Him helps us to actually do it. How goal-oriented are you?

Read 1 Thessalonians 4:13-18

For the Lord himself will come down from heaven, with a loud command, with the voice of the archangel and with the trumpet call of God, and the dead in Christ will rise first. After that, we who are still alive will be caught up together with them in the clouds to meet the Lord in the air, and so we will be with the Lord forever.

1 Thessalonians 4:16, 17

Ninth inning —

READY POSITION

IT IS ESPECIALLY IMPORTANT for a baseball player to have his body in a ready position prior to a pitch. All infielders must have their weight evenly distributed on the balls of their feet. They must have knees flexed, head up, and hands off their knees. They are not to be resting, but to be ready for sudden, instantaneous action!

Believers in Jesus are to be in a spiritual "ready" position. According to Jesus promise, Christians are to be ready for a sudden, instantaneous removal from this world! On the night before He was crucified, Jesus promised to personally come again for us (John 14:1-3). He told John that He'd come soon (Revelation 22:12). We will be quickly "caught up" into the clouds to be with Jesus forever! The description indicated we are "seized" or "snatched" with a powerful, irresistible force. Like a magnet attracting iron filings, or like a powerful vacuum cleaner, Jesus will catch us away to meet Him in the clouds!

Though there are no signs preceding this event, we need not be surprised. Believers see Him in the clouds, He shouts a command of joy and triumph, and the archangel (Michael) blows a trumpet blast. There is no time for Satan, the ruler of the kingdom of the air (Ephesians 2:2) to overcome us as we rendezvous with Jesus above the earth! He is restrained while we pass by!

Though this not the end of the world (Jesus later comes to *earth* to set up His government — Matthew 24:29, 30; Revelation 19:11-16), we will be with Jesus forever!

Believers in Thessalonica were concerned about loved ones who had died. Paul said to not grieve or sorrow like unbelievers who have no hope. Their funerals are full of stoic indifference or wails of extreme grief. The bodies of lost people return to dust and their souls go to a place of torment (Luke 16). But while the bodies of believers return to dust, their souls go to be with Jesus immediately (Luke 23:43; 2 Corinthians 5:8). Early Christians called burial grounds "cemeteries," a Greek word meaning "dormitory" or "sleeping chamber." The Christian's body sleeps until resurrected to be made like His glorious body (1 John 3:2; Philippians 3:21). We won't be a vapor, a mist, or a ghost, but a tangible, material, physical body with our redeemed souls and able to do supernatural things!

Are you in a spiritual "ready" position? We don't know when He will come (Acts 1:7) but we'd better be "on our toes" in ready position. The move we make will be very quick!

Read Thessalonians 5:1-11

Now, brothers, about times and dates we do not need to write to you, for you know very well that the day of the Lord will come like a thief in the night.

1 Thessalonians 5:1, 2

Ninth inning—
DAY OF THE LORD

ALL WINTER LONG, baseball fans anticipate opening day of the new season. They discuss the next pennant race in their "Hot Stove Leagues." Players lift weights and run to condition their bodies for the demands of the long, hot summer. Executives wheel and deal in hopes of acquiring the best players. There is much anticipation as a dignitary throws out the first pitch on opening day and the season begins.

Paul anticipates that Jesus Christ will "throw out the first pitch" on a new season when He appears in the clouds to gather believers to Himself. This new season, called the "day of the Lord," is discussed more than any other time period (95 times) in Scripture. Yet, no one knows when this season will open (Acts 1:7; 1 Thessalonians 5:1, 2)! This season is a time of great suffering (Tribulation) followed by great blessing (Millennium). Let's examine the characteristics of the "day of the Lord."

In the Old Testament, Joel (2:28-32) warned of a great and dreadful day of the Lord. He said there would be deliverance from Jerusalem only for survivors whom God will call. Daniel (12:1) warned of a time of great distress on earth and deliverance for some of the Jews. Jeremiah (30:7) speaks of a time of trouble and salvation for Jacob (Jews). Isaiah (2:10-22, 12:1-22, 34:1-8) describes the day of the Lord as a dreadful day of God's judgment on Israel and all nations. He also speaks of a mighty God who tramples the nations in His wrath (63:1-6). Zechariah (14:1-21) says there will be terrible violence and warfare followed by God's sovereign rule over the whole world. Zephaniah (1:14-18) describes a bloody day of fire and wrath.

In the New Testament, Jesus described a great tribulation (Matthew 24) — the worst time to ever come upon the world. Peter (2 Peter 3:1-13) says the day of the Lord comes suddenly with much destruction as the elements melt! John (Revelation 6-19) describes this period in graphic detail.

No one knows when this "season" will open. Much talk of peace and safety precedes it, however (v 3). We do know that Jesus Christ will return for His people. So we stay on the alert (v 6). We await His glorious appearing (Titus 2:13). We are to be rescued from the coming wrath (1 Thessalonians 1:10, 5:9)! What a glorious promise! What an encouragement (v 11). It's one season we'll be glad to miss!

Read 1 Thessalonians 5:12-28

May God himself, the God of peace, sanctify you through and through. May your whole spirit, soul, and body be kept blameless at the coming of our Lord Jesus Christ.

1 Thessalonians 5:23

Ninth inning —
LAST-MINUTE INSTRUCTIONS

AS A FOOTBALL COACH prepares his team to take the field each week, he always gives last-minute instructions. It's a time when team unity should be at its peak as all face a common opponent. Usually, the coach simply repeats the tactics most crucial to victory that have been presented all week.

As Paul closed his first letter, he listed crucial, last-minute instructions to believers as they await the return of Jesus. He listed the most essential tactics of walking with God. Twenty-two commands are given to those who love Jesus. They are listed briefly like a military code of conduct. These ethics are a higher standard than the Ten Commandments, an Old Testament system given so we would see our sin and know we needed the death of Jesus to save us (Romans 7).

We can almost hear coach Paul enthusiastically reminding the Thessalonians to honor and respect their pastors because of their vital roles, to warn the "idle" (a military term describing soldiers who failed to stay in the ranks), to encourage the timid, to help the weak, to return good for evil, and to be kind to everyone. We are to be joyful (an inward quality not dependent on outward circumstances) always, to pray (maintain conversation with God) constantly, and to give thanks in *all* circumstances (we never have a reason to complain against God).

We must not "put out the Spirit's fire" by withholding fuel (God's Word) or by putting dirt (unclean lifestyles) in it! We quench God's Spirit by not doing as He directs

117

and acting independently. We are to respect prophecies of pastors, but not be naïve, taken in by flattery, deceit, and religious rackets. We must examine (test) everything in the light of God's Word. We must avoid evil and cling to the good.

As we follow these commands, our God keeps us *blameless* until He comes. Notice, we are not *sinless*, for the Bible says those who claim sinlessness are self-deceived (1 John 1:8). But we can live in such a way that no man can point an accusing finger and blame us for causing him to stumble. We can be good role models!

The last-minute words of a coach are usually the most significant. They are meant to keep the team focused on the goal. As we obey the final words of Paul's letter, may we remain focused upon Jesus Christ, the coming King of Kings!

Introduction
Second Thessalonians

QUESTIONS AROSE in the minds of the new Christians in Thessalonica after reading Paul's first letter. So, he wrote a second one a few months later. A false letter, which stated that Christ had already come and snatched believers out of this world, was being circulated among the people. Some believers had quit their jobs in expectation of Christ's return! Because they were suffering persecution, it was easy to believe they were in the "Great Tribulation" and the "Day of the Lord." Paul wrote to acknowledge their suffering, but also to assure them they had not missed Jesus' coming. He wrote to distinguish between the "catching away" of believers (the "rapture") when Jesus comes in the air *for* his people, and the time when Jesus comes to earth *with* his people to judge evildoers and set up his kingdom (the "revelation" of Jesus). Paul indicated that certain forerunners (a great apostasy in churches and the appearance of a "man of sin") must come before the "day of the Lord."

Since Paul's day, many suffering Christians have believed they were in the Great Tribulation Period. For example, many British ministries believed they had entered it during World War II. Because all who live godly lives in Christ will suffer (2 Timothy 3:12), it is easy for us to think the Tribulation has begun. But the Great Tribulation is still future. All other suffering is on a small scale in comparison! After that period, Jesus will establish His kingdom on earth. The revelation of Jesus in judgment of unbelievers and in righteous rule is still to come in the future. What a great day that will be!

Read 2 Thessalonians 1:1-12

God is just: He will pay back trouble to those who trouble you and give relief to you who are troubled, and to us as well. This will happen when the Lord Jesus is revealed from heaven in blazing fire with his powerful angels.

2 Thessalonians 1:6, 7

Ninth inning —
PAYBACK TIME:
THE REVELATION OF JESUS

SOME PRO ATHLETES have long memories when an opponent takes a cheap shot at them on the field, court or ice. Hockey players wait months or years for just the right moment to take revenge on an enemy. Some football players take mental notes of cheap shots and do the same. In baseball, a pitcher is sometimes ordered by his manager to "pay back" the other team by hitting someone when one of his teammates has been hit.

Revenge is common in the athletic world. It is man's feeble effort to find justice in an unjust world, but it is to be reserved for God alone. Romans 12:19 says, "Do not take revenge, my friends, but leave room for God's wrath, for it is written: 'It is mine to avenge; I will repay,' says the Lord."

As the believers in Thessalonica learned more about Jesus Christ, their faith grew by leaps and bounds! It flourished like green plants in the tropics. Much rain (persecution) and much sun (the love of God) produced much growth (love for others). Because they didn't run from suffering, their patience and hope in the future was greatly increased (Romans 5:3-5).

Paul wrote his second letter to encourage Christians that justice at the hand of God was on the way! He described the revelation of Jesus Christ as "payback time" for both the godly and the ungodly. While it is wrong for us to seek revenge, the justice of God *de-*

mands that wickedness be punished and righteousness rewarded. He will punish those who don't know God and those who refused the gospel (v 8). The former didn't think God was worth knowing (Romans 1:28), while the latter loved their sin more than the Savior (John 3:17-21). Our God will punish evil, but not vindictively. He judges sinners to vindicate His righteousness and holiness. If evil were not punished, God would not be just, for sin is absolutely detestable and intolerable to our holy God. If man clings to his sin, he *must* be judged. Oliver Greene says, "To bring peace, rest, and relaxation to the righteous is the common rule of justice with God; to bring misery, anguish, woe, and torment to the wicked and upon those who hate God is also the common rule of justice with God."

It is a dreadful thing to fall into the hands of the living God (Hebrews 10:31). Psalm 9:17 says, "The wicked return to the grave, all the nations that forget God." (This includes the USA, by the way.) God will terrify the scoffers who thought He was too weak to rule (Psalm 2). He will divide the righteous from the unrighteous (Matthew 25:31-46). While heaven is better than our wildest dreams, hell is much more terrible than our worst nightmare. It is likened to a fiery furnace where there is weeping and gnashing of teeth (Matthew 13:42). It is a lake of fire (Revelation 20:15) and darkness (Matthew 25:30). Those who think they will party with friends are dreadfully mistaken, for it is a place of terrible isolation from all that is good. It is an eternally hopeless place where one is forever consciously aware of suffering.

How contrasting is God's "payback" to believers in Jesus. We will be amazed when He is glorified in us like the sun in a mirror (v 10). When He is revealed to set up His earthly kingdom, it will be a great honor to be the "bride" (church) married to our husband (Jesus), who loved us enough to die for us! We will rule with Him (Revelation 20:4) as He rules with an iron scepter (Revelation 19:15).

Christian, you may be in the minority now — but you are on the winning team! It will take the dramatic revelation of Jesus Christ Himself to straighten out this world — but He will come! Suffering drives our roots deeper into the bedrock of His love for us. Because of His great salvation and His just judgment, we are greatly encouraged to live lives which please Him. Come, Lord Jesus!

Read 2 Thessalonians 2:1-4

*He will oppose and will exalt himself over everything that is
called God or is worshipped, so that he sets himself up in God's
temple, proclaiming himself to be God.*

2 Thessalonians 2:4

Ninth inning —
THE MAN OF LAWLESSNESS

ON OCTOBER 26, 1912, just prior to Georgia's first play
against Alabama, end Alonzo Autrey stood near the
sidelines dressed in coveralls and holding a bucket. The
Tide assumed he was the water boy. When the ball was
snapped, Autrey sped downfield and caught a long pass.
Angry Alabama rooters charged Bulldog fans and police
had to break up a brawl. Georgia went on to a 13-9
victory as referees let the play stand.

Just as Alonzo Autrey deceived the entire Alabama
team, a day will come when one man will deceive the
whole world! Paul calls him the "man of lawlessness."
John calls him the antichrist (1 John 2:18-22). Scripture gives him over 30 similar titles such as "beast,"
"man of sin," and "another king." His rule will be a time
of terrible suffering for everyone alive. In fact, during his
rule a large percentage of the world's population will be
killed, either by judgments from heaven or by the brutal
slaughter of his forces. This is the time period called the
Great Tribulation.

Believers in Thessalonica were suffering for their
faith. Someone had evidently written a letter telling
them they were in this time period and forged Paul's
name to it (2:1, 2). They worried they had missed the
rapture of the church! This false teaching discouraged
them, robbed them of their missionary zeal, and left
them in constant agitation. To correct their misunder-
standing, Paul wrote that two things must happen
before the day of the Lord would occur. First, a rebellion
("revolt" or "defection from the faith") would occur. This

125

includes denial of the fundamentals of Jesus' virgin birth, miracles, atonement for sin, His bodily resurrection, and His second coming. Apostasy which denies the inerrancy of God's Word has been around almost from the beginning, but total, worldwide apostasy in the organized church will precede the Great Tribulation (Luke 18:8). This "world church" is the harlot of Revelation 17. When the rapture takes place, only unsaved church people are left to make up this religious group. Secondly, the "man of lawlessness" is revealed. This deceiver establishes an empire in Western Europe (Revelation 13), abolishes all religion, and demands worship of himself. He sets himself up in God's temple (evidently it is rebuilt in Jerusalem) and claims to be God! He is, in fact, Satan in the flesh. For three and one-half terrible years the deception continues. The man of lawlessness is the ultimate in self-deification.

Deception is nothing new. Neither is discouragement. But we can be encouraged to know that our gathering to Jesus must be soon. We will never be deceived by the man of lawlessness.

Read 2 Thessalonians 2:5-12

For the secret power of lawlessness is already at work; but the one who now holds it back will continue to do so till he is taken out of the way.

2 Thessalonians 2:7

Ninth inning —
PULLING OUT ALL THE STOPS

WE LIVE IN A WORLD of lawlessness, lust, and greed. Even such occasions as the 1993 "three-peat" by the Chicago Bulls resulted in 2 deaths, dozens of injuries, and hundreds of arrests in the "victory celebration" that followed. Magic Johnson lived in sexual sin and contacted AIDS, joining thousands of others who degrade their bodies sexually and with drugs. Mike Tyson, who enjoys money and fame, sexually abused a beauty contestant and went to prison. The immorality of athletes and fans pollutes the sports pages every day.

Though many people have no time for God today, the Holy Spirit still is restraining evil. He is present in Christians to motivate them, providing salt and light to society. Imagine what life would be like without Him. One day, perhaps soon, the Christians will be "caught up" to meet Jesus in the air (1 Thessalonians 4:16-18). The Spirit will then stop restraining evil. Because the people still on earth loved darkness rather than light (John 3:19), God will give them what they crave — a world without His light. Because people reject the truth ("Jesus is Lord"), God sends them a powerful delusion ("Antichrist is Lord") to reveal all that is in their wicked hearts. He will finally "give them over to their own lusts" (Romans 1). The judgment of God will fall on an unbelieving world, as the "lawless one" is revealed and all the "stops" are removed. With supernatural signs, wonders and miracles (v 9), the antichrist will cause people to believe he is the Messiah and that they are headed into a glorious time of peace without the Christians. Instead,

127

they enter the Great Tribulation Period. All past suffering on this planet will seem as child's play, as people who have stood for nothing fall for anything.

God has a purpose for bringing antichrist on the scene. He will show that those who reject Jesus Christ (truth) will accept a bloody and deceitful antichrist. Therefore, God is fully justified in judging sinners and assigning them to the hell they have chosen.

At the end of the Great Tribulation Period, Jesus will come to earth to reign (Daniel 7:13, 14). The Lord said this would be a worldwide rule of power and great glory (Matthew 24:27-30)! He will lead Heaven's armies (angels and saints) to claim the earth. A sharp sword coming out of His mouth will destroy the armies of the world, which have been assembled by Satan (Revelation 19:11-18). The devil, the "beast" (a dictator who rules through a European alliance), and the false prophet (antichrist aligned with the beast) are eventually cast into a lake of burning sulfur to be tormented forever (Revelation 20:10).

Yes, all the stops will be pulled out. There will be a "hell on earth." But that time will be a short three and one-half years. Jesus will return to establish His kingdom and righteousness will rule. Praise His Holy Name!

Read 2 Thessalonians 2:13-17

*So then, brothers, stand firm and hold to the teachings we
passed on to you, whether by word of mouth or by letter.*
2 Thessalonians 2:15

Ninth inning —
Standing Firm

GOOD COACHING is essential to the maximum development of athletes. But is one thing to listen to good
instruction, and quite another to put it into practice.
Often, old habits must be broken before new skills are
learned. The process can be difficult, but if a player
doesn't apply what he is taught he might as well not
have even heard the new information.

The Thessalonian Christians had received good
coaching from Paul. But because of the daily pressures
of their trials and the pull of the world, the flesh, and
the devil, they (and we) were in constant danger of being
swept downstream by the currents of an ungodly culture. They needed to guard their relationship with God
from a cold deadness and to stand firm in the instruction Paul had imparted.

Why stand firm in the "coaching" of Paul? Because,
like the Thessalonians, we are loved by the Lord (v 13).
He took the initiative to save us because of His great
love for us! He *chose* us to be saved through the work of
the Holy Spirit and our belief in the truth by the gospel
Paul preached (vv 13, 14). It is His plan that we share
His glory (v 14). But the only way we can reflect that
glory to others is to stand firm in God's Word, keeping
our eyes on Jesus instead of the wickedness around us.

Our God is a great Encourager. Paul says He gave us
"eternal encouragement" in every good deed and word
(vv 16, 17). It is He who gave us faith (2 Peter 1:1) in the
beginning and it is He who provides it to the end. Our
duty is to believe Him and to stand firm — no matter
what happens.

Read 2 Thessalonians 3:1-18

For even when we were with you, we gave you this rule: "If a man will not work, he shall not eat."

2 Thessalonians 3:10

Ninth inning —

Get Busy

NO ATHLETE will ever become all he could be if he stops working hard to improve. He must keep an emphasis upon achievement as he wrestles with the problems of his profession. At this writing, Jerry Rice is the NFL's all-time leader with 103 TD catches. He didn't become a great receiver by talent alone. Michael Carter, 49er nose tackle, said of Rice, "It's his work ethic. All the things he's achieved, we can see the hard work he's put into it."

After Paul requested prayer for himself and for the spread of the gospel (3:1-5), he warned the Thessalonians to "get busy" in maintaining a good work ethic. Idleness is not a godly trait, and some people had become lazy in the belief that Jesus was coming soon and the world would end. Able-bodied men were actually being taken care of by the working believers! This brought dishonor to the Lord and discredited the gospel message. Paul told working believers to stay away from them (not to give them money) in hopes they would be shamed into repentance.

Those who really believe Jesus is coming soon will maintain a good work ethic, both in their secular jobs and in sharing the gospel. They know friends need to be saved. They know we will be judged for rewards based upon our faithfulness. And they know time is limited. Paul was an example of hard work. When he spent three weeks teaching new converts in Thessalonica, he worked night and day as a tentmaker to support himself. This highly-educated Roman citizen was never influenced by Roman and Greek philosophy that regarded manual labor as degrading and fit only for slaves. He followed the Hebrew custom of learning a trade and set an industrious example.

Even before Adam, the first man, fell into sin, he was held responsible by God to cultivate ("dress") and protect ("keep") the Garden of Eden. A good work ethic is not only a key to reaching our potential in sports, but also is pleasing to God. Let's get busy as we wait for Jesus to return!

God's Extra inning —

A STUDY OF

THE REVELATION OF

JESUS CHRIST

The Real One . . .

JESUS CHRIST

Inning	1	2	3	4	5	6	7	8	9	10
SATAN	0	Fall	0	0	Slavery	Captivity	Crucifixion	Suffering	Deception	Tribulation
GOD	Creation	Promise	Flood	Abraham	Israel	David	Resurrection	Spirit	Rapture	Millennium

How They Scored

Tenth inning —

Antichrist is given control of earth . . . Man's evil nature does its
worst . . . millions are murdered . . . earth's worst time in history . . .
King Jesus appears . . . destroys the armies of the world . . . casts
Satan into the Abyss . . . reigns in peace and righteousness for 1000
years . . . releases Satan for one last rally . . . Satan is captured and
cast into burning sulphur forever, along with all unbelievers . . . New
heaven and new earth . . . eternity . . . God wins!

Read Revelation 1:1-8

*Look, he is coming with the clouds, and every eye will see him,
even those who pierced him; and all the people of the earth will
mourn because of him. So shall it be! Amen.*

Revelation 1:7

Tenth inning —
THE PROMISE OF HIS RETURN

WHEN GENERAL DOUGLAS MacARTHUR withdrew
from the Philippines after the bombing of Pearl Harbor,
he issued his brief and famous statement: "I will return."
For several years, millions of people in the Orient hung
onto those three words in the midst of the totalitarian
oppression of cruel and ungodly forces. They were words
of hope. Finally, MacArthur *did* return to free the Philippines! And he did not stop in Manila. He went on to
Tokyo to receive the surrender of the proud Japanese on
the deck of the battleship *Missouri.* Though a frail human, MacArthur kept his promise. He did return!

Before Jesus Christ left this earth to return to
heaven, He promised, "I will come again" (John 14:3).
We do not know when He will return, but we know our
wonderful Savior *will keep* His promise. He said He
would come quickly (Revelation 22:12). He did not say
He would come "soon," though it could be very soon. He
indicated that His coming and all events involved would
occupy a very brief time. More is being understood today
concerning His return, and mankind will see more truth
unfold as we near the grand event. We are "hikers," not
"campers," in this life, so we cannot "camp" on any
doctrine. But the *fact* of His coming is a great encouragement!

Daniel (7:13, 14) prophesied that Jesus would set up
a sovereign kingdom over all people of the earth. Zechariah (12:10) said that the Jews would finally recognize
Jesus, the One they had crucified, as their King (14:9).
But the major revelation of Revelation is that "every eye

135

will see Him" (1:8). The whole world will see Jesus —
alive and coming in great glory to rule the earth. He will
return! Much to the despair of all who reject Him and
the joy of those who love Him, our Lord Jesus will reign
over the earth!

Come quickly, Lord Jesus!.

Read Revelation 1:9-20

*I am the Living One; I was dead, and behold I am alive for ever
and ever! And I hold the keys of death and Hades. Write,
therefore, what you have seen, what is now, and what will
take place later.*

Revelation 1:18, 19

Tenth inning —
Vision of Greatness

A VISION of what is possible is a great motivator for a
team or an individual. Without a goal or a vision we
become listless, lethargic, and demotivated. But where
there are clear goals and a strong assurance of success,
teams and people are empowered. What many teams
(and people) lack is a revelation of how good they can
become!

Patmos was a rugged, volcanic island in the Mediter-
ranean, 10 miles long and 6 miles wide. In ancient
times, it was used by the Romans as a prison. The
apostle John, formerly a pastor in Ephesus, was exiled
to slave labor in the mines of Patmos by the cruel em-
peror Domitian. During his bleakest days, John had a
God-given revelation of future world events. According to
verse 19, John saw and was told to write (1) what he
had seen, (2) what is now, and (3) what will take place
later. This verse is the key to understanding the entire
book of Revelation. "What he had seen" was the glorified
Christ (Chapter 1)! "What is now" is the churches (Chapters 2-3). "What will take place later" is God's program of
judgment after the true believers in Jesus Christ are
removed from earth (Chapters 4-22).

In Chapter 1, John saw the glorified Jesus! However,
He was not the pale, meek, mild, cultural icon many of
us picture! He spoke with a *loud* voice, like a trumpet (v
10) or like rushing water (v 15). A trumpet blast or the
roar of Niagara Falls speaks of authority and power. The
long robe with a golden sash around His chest speaks of

137

His inherent righteousness. His hair, white as wool or snow, speaks of His eternal existence. Jesus sees everything we do with eyes of flaming fire. How careful we must be to obey His will, knowing He is watching! His face was brilliant in strength and splendor. His feet, like bronze, symbolize judgment — for He is ready to trample the winepress of God's wrath upon a Christ-rejecting world. The seven stars in His right hand symbolize His control of the universe. The sword coming from His mouth pictures the Word of God by which He will judge the earth. Heaven and earth will pass away, but God's Word will never pass away (Mark 13:31). His face is like the sun. Man can't look at the sun directly, so how could he look at the Creator who made the sun? When Paul saw Him (Acts 9:4-9) he was blinded for three days.

What an awesome scene John saw! The only possible reaction to the appearance of Jesus Christ is to fall at His feet as though dead (v 17). John had been close friends with Jesus at the Lord's first coming. Now, he is paralyzed at His glorified appearance. Now, he falls at His feet!

What did the Savior say to John? He said, "Do not be afraid." Why should John (and we) not fear? We fear not because He is the First and the Last, the Eternal One, the Creator and Finisher of all things. We fear not because He is now alive. He conquered our worst enemy — death! We fear not because He holds the keys of death and Hades. He controls our destiny! Hades (Greek: "unseen world") could mean the physical grave or where the spirit goes at death. Jesus controls both! What a vision of who He really is! What encouragement and direction He gives as we pursue His will!

Read Revelation 4

You are worthy, our Lord and God, to receive glory and honor and power, for you created all things, and by your will they were created and have their being.

Revelation 4:11

Tenth inning —
MEGAWORSHIP

SPORTS INFORMATION DIRECTORS have the responsibility to declare the worth of great players and teams. They publish press guides to promote their team to the media. Sometimes they produce posters of great players, touting them as All-Americans or Heisman Trophy candidates. It is the job of the SID to declare the worth of those who represent their school.

The worship of God is the highest activity in which man can be engaged. Yet, A. W. Tozer calls worship "the missing jewel of the evangelical church." Sometimes, we are not very good "information directors" about God! We have not yet learned to worship ("to declare God's worth") adequately. In Revelation 4, John was "airlifted" to heaven, where he caught a glimpse of the main activity there: the declaration of God's worth.

After believers in Jesus are removed from the earth (1 Thessalonians 4:13-18), they will be found in heaven. During the Great Tribulation Period (Revelation 6-19), there is no mention of the true church on the earth. It is this removal of the Spirit and of all true believers (now called the bride of Christ in Heaven) that opens the door for Satan to take complete control of earth through sinful man. God will allow man to fully reveal his true nature. But Revelation 4 describes a Heavenly scene — worship of God as Creator. Let's see what John was shown!

John saw a throne (symbol of authority and power) occupied by Someone with the crystal clear brilliance of jasper (God's holiness) and the deep red of carnelian

(Jesus' blood atonement). An emerald rainbow (recalling God's eternal power, grace, and mercy to Noah and all creation) encircled His throne, from which came thunder and lightning (denoting the judgment of God ready to fall on a Christ-rejecting world). Seven lamps, representing the completeness of God's Holy Spirit and a crystal clear (peaceful) sea of glass were before God's throne.

Four living creatures gave glory, honor and thanks to God day and night. The noble lionlike creature reflects God's majesty and power. The oxlike creature reflects God's strength and patience. The manlike creature reflects God's reason and intelligence. The eaglelike creature reflects God's swift majesty and keen alertness. All give Him glory!

Twenty-four elders sitting on thrones surrounding God's throne are dressed in white and wearing crowns ("Stephanoi"). Stephanoi were rewards bestowed on winners of ancient Greek athletic contests. These elders have run the great race of faith, been rewarded, and now worship God by continually removing their crowns and placing them at His feet!

What a scene! And what a future for the believer in Jesus! Are you ready to worship? Do you worship Him now by giving Him credit for all your awards? He created you, He redeemed you, and He alone is worthy of our worship.

Read Revelation 5

And they sang a new song:
    You are worthy to take the scroll and to open its seals,
because you were slain, and with your blood you purchased
men for God from every tribe and language and people and
nation. You have made them to be a kingdom and priests to
serve our God, and they will reign on the earth.

Revelation 5:9, 10

Tenth inning —
WHEN JESUS OPENS HIS MOUTH

PROUD AND ARROGANT MEN are often filled with "hot air" in spouting their own ability and strength. Nowhere is this seen more than in the athletic world. The finger-pointing and taunting that had to be banned in college football was ruining the game for spectators! No one appreciates cocky arrogance, especially when the athlete may fall down and be embarrassed a few plays later.

Jesus Christ is not a loud-mouthed braggart breathing hot air. When Jesus opens His mouth, all heaven and earth pay attention. While on earth Jesus opened His mouth and taught simple, yet profound truths about God and what He expects from men. People listened. When He went to the cross, He "opened not his mouth" (Isaiah 53:7), but willingly paid the price for our sins. Now, Jesus sits at the right hand of the Majesty in Heaven (Hebrews 1;3). But in Revelation 5 (a continuation of chapter 4), John saw Him as a Lamb *standing* in the center of the throne. The Father held a seven-sealed scroll, representing the title deed to the earth, but no one was found in heaven, on earth, or under the earth who was worthy to open the seals or look inside. John wept and wept at the thought that no one was competent to overthrow Satan's stranglehold on earth, remove the curse of sin, and rule the world. Then Jesus, the lamb still bearing the marks of His death on the cross, took the scroll from God's right hand. As a Lamb, He must have *opened His mouth* to take the scroll! His seven horns and seven eyes depict His total power and complete knowledge. He is now standing (Isaiah 3:13) ready, willing, and able to open the scroll to reveal the judgments He will pour out on earth during the Tribulation Period (Revelation 6-19). The scroll is the key which opens the door to these chapters.

A new song (vs 9, 10) is sung to Him. This is a song of His redemption of mankind by the blood of His cross. Today, man is taking songs about Jesus' blood out of some denominational hymnbooks. But in Heaven, elders, living creatures, and angels all sing about His blood. The old song of His creation (Job 38:7) was glorious, but this new song of redemption brings even more praise to the Lamb. He created the world, He redeemed it, and He is worthy to rule it. He alone has met the conditions of our salvation!

In Revelation 19:11-21, Jesus appears on a white stallion, leading the armies of Heaven to take over the rulership of earth. All He must do is open His mouth (from which comes a sharp sword) and the war is over! He completely overwhelms the enemies of God by His Word! What a wonderful and powerful Savior! Praise His Holy Name!

Read Revelation 6-18

For then there will be great distress, unequaled from the beginning of the world until now — and never to be equaled again. If those days had not been cut short, no one would survive, but for the sake of the elect those days will be shortened.
Matthew 24:21, 22

Tenth inning —
THE GREAT TRIBULATION

THE 1939 ORANGE BOWL was the roughest, no-holds barred Bowl game ever. The Tennessee Volunteers and the Oklahoma Sooners threw fists and curses on almost every play. A record 221 yards in penalties were assessed, including nine for unnecessary roughness. Even a cheerleader was bowled over and knocked out during the brutal contest.

There is coming upon the world a brief time (3 1/2 years) of suffering which will make the most brutal football game seem like a Sunday School picnic. Though no one understands every detail, men have known of such a time since the days of Daniel (Daniel 7-12). The prophet Jeremiah also predicted a "time of Jacob's (Jewish) trouble" (Jeremiah 30:5-7). Joel said only a remnant would be saved out of terrible judgment (Joel 2-3). Jesus' words (Matthew 24) and John's vision (Revelation 6-18) greatly expanded our knowledge. In the revelation to John, God revealed seven seal judgments, followed by seven trumpet judgments, followed by seven bowl judgments — each increasing in severity. Between the description of each are inserted chapters 7, 10-11:14, 12-14, and 17:19:10 which deal with individuals and situations but do not advance the narrative.

According to Daniel 9, a ruler will sign a seven-year ("one week" of years) peace pact for the protection of Israel. After three and one-half years, this "beast" (who is energized by Satan) will break the agreement and begin persecuting the Jews (Matthew 24:15) and anyone else who rejects his authority. Revelation 6 begins the account of this false Messiah taking peace from the earth for the remaining three and one-half years. According to Jesus, unless these days were brief, no one would survive. A second beast commands worship from the world (Revelation 13), as the world government exerts political, economic, military, and religious control. Jews who finally recognize Jesus as the true Messiah are martyred. They are the fortunate ones.

Millions are slain as God pours out His righteous wrath on an unbelieving world. Hail, fire and blood fall, one-third of sea life is destroyed, and one-third of the sun, moon and stars are darkened (Revelation 8). Bizarre locusts torment men and millions die in terrible torment (Revelation 9). Mankind still refuses to repent of sins against a holy God (vs 20, 21). As earthquakes, more hail, plagues, fire and war continue, man curses God further (16:9, 11, 21). Only the glorious appearance of Jesus (Revelation 19) will stop the carnage. He who has the right to rule assumes control and binds Satan for 1000 years.

What are the lessons of the Great Tribulation? First, God does punish sin. His patience has a limit as He pours out His righteous wrath on ungodly men. Secondly, even the worst of times does not reform man's evil heart. He clings to his idolatry, murder, magic arts, sexual immorality and thefts (9:20, 21). He is not subject to rehabilitation. Only the blood of Jesus washes away sin and changes a life. Thirdly, there are absolutes of right and wrong. Whether man believes them or not, God enforces them. He is not mocked. Fourth, God is greatly to be feared by unbelievers who ignore or disobey Him. His wrath is terrible.

If you have repented of your sin and trusted Jesus, you have nothing to fear. The church is not mentioned in Revelation 6-18, having been snatched away! But for those who refuse to repent, a hellish future is coming — possibly very soon.

Read Revelation 19:1-10

Then I heard what sounded like a great multitude, like the roar of rushing water and like loud peals of thunder, shouting: "Hallelujah! For our Lord God Almighty reigns. Let us rejoice and be glad and give him glory! For the wedding of the Lamb has come, and his bride has made herself ready. Fine linen, bright and clean, was given her to wear." (Fine linen stands for the righteous acts of the saints.)

Revelation 19:6-8

Tenth inning —
THE GREATEST WEDDING IN HISTORY

AFTER THE TRIBULATION PERIOD on earth (Revelation 6-18), John heard the praise of God by all creatures in Heaven! Jesus is about to judge the world and to establish his 1000-year millennial kingdom (Acts 17:31)! He is going to fulfill the prayer He taught us to pray: ". . . your kingdom come, your will be done on earth as it is in heaven" (Matthew 6:10)! He is going to rule the earth, and His bride (true believers) will rule with Him. The groan of creation as it awaits this day (Romans 8:18-23) will turn into praise as Jesus Christ returns to conquer the world and throw Satan into the "Abyss." The Son of David (Jesus) fulfills God's promise to David, "Your house and your kingdom will endure forever before me; your throne will be established forever" (2 Samuel 7:16). The government will be upon His shoulder (Isaiah 9:6, 7). His kingdom will never end (Luke 1:31-33)!

A first-century wedding included (1) the legal consummation of the transaction by payment of a dowry (Jesus paid in blood for our salvation), (2) the coming of the groom to claim the bride (Christ will take His bride to heaven), and (3) the wedding feast, a supper that lasted several days (We return to earth to reign with Him!). Only two events precede His rule. First, the false religious, political, and economic systems of this world (Babylon) must be destroyed. The harlot (false religion)

145

is judged in Chapter 18 of Revelation. Secondly, the marriage of Jesus (the Lamb) and His bride (true believes must take place in heaven. This happens after the rapture and our appearance before His judgment seat. Then Jesus and His bride return to earth to reign. The harlot and the bride cannot occupy the same scene at the same time.

God, in His grace, makes us ready to rule with Him (Colossians 1:12). He gives us the robe of His righteousness (Romans 3:21, 2 Corinthians 5:21) in exchange for our filthy rags (Isaiah 64:6). But we also prepare ourselves by abiding in Him (1 John 2:28). At His judgment seat, all our wasted time, missed opportunities, and unfaithfulness are burned as dross from fine gold (2 Corinthians 5:10). Many lazy, indifferent believers will be sorrowful before they are ready to return to earth to rule with Him (1 Corinthians 3:10-15). Faithful believers will be rewarded. All believers will stand in fine linen, symbolic of righteous acts (v 8) before returning to earth for the marriage supper (Millennium) with Jesus and His friends (Old Testament believers).

Jesus is given thunderous praise by all creation because He has purchased His bride and will conquer the earth! The worship is loud and long, in a sound previously unheard by human ears! His righteousness, holiness, and truth are worthy of praise, for surely He can do no wrong! All of His dealings with His creatures —whether in grace or in judgment — are absolutely right! What a glorious time to be with Him! The best is yet to come! How great to be a child of the King

Read Revelation 19:11-21

At that time the sign of the Son of Man will appear in the sky, and all the nations of the earth will mourn. They will see the Son of Man coming on the clouds of the sky with power and great glory.

Matthew 24:30

Tenth inning —
THE GREAT RELIEF APPEARANCE

GREAT RELIEF PITCHERS have become extremely valuable to professional baseball teams. The job has become such an art that any team expecting to win many games must have excellent long (middle inning) and short (late inning) relievers. When the starting pitcher falters and a crisis develops, smart managers have a systematic relief plan to control the enemy rally.

At the end of the coming worldwide crisis (Great Tribulation), Jesus Christ will make the greatest "relief appearance" of all time! His second coming has been prophesied for thousands of years. His appearance as a mighty Warrior, Judge, and King is the focal point of prophecy. Daniel foretold His coming as King even before He came as Savior the first time (Daniel 7:13, 14). Many Psalms (22, 24, 50, 72, 96, and 110) predict His coming and the kingdom He will establish. Throughout the Old Testament, prophets connected Christ's coming with His reign over the nations from the throne of David (Zechariah 14).

For centuries, men have scoffed at Him, asking, "Where is the promise of His coming?" (2 Peter 3:4). Their ridicule will cease abruptly. As Satan marshals the armies of the world at Armageddon (Revelation 16:12-16), Jesus appears in majesty upon a white horse. The world's armies (under Antichrist) unite to fight against the Lord Jesus (Revelation 19:11-21). Psalm 2 prophesies their futility! With justice and judgment He makes war on them all! Jesus destroys them with the "breath of his mouth" (Isaiah 11:4). The same powerful word that spoke creation into existence annihilates the armies of this rebellious planet! Revelation 19:15 describes it as a "sharp sword coming out of his mouth" with which He strikes down the nations. Those who have rejected His mercy suffer His wrath. The strength and pride of the nations becomes fodder for vultures, as birds of prey gorge themselves on their flesh. The beast and his false prophet are thrown alive into a lake of burning sulfur, and Satan is chained in the abyss for 1000 years during Jesus' earthly reign (Millennium).

What is our part in this war? Believers of this age, having been raptured earlier, return with Jesus (armies of heaven) riding white horses and clothed in white. There will be thousands upon thousands of us (Jude 14,15). Whoever heard of an army clothed in white? No one. But we do not fight! One word from Jesus is all it takes to overwhelm His enemies! He comes in holy vengeance to trod upon all who have rejected Him — and He needs none of our help (Isaiah 63:1-6). What a relief appearance! What a King!

Read Revelation 20:1-6

The infant will play near the hole of the cobra, and the young child put his hand into the viper's nest. They will neither harm nor destroy on all my holy mountain, for the earth will be full of the knowledge of the Lord as the waters cover the sea.

Isaiah 11:8, 9

Tenth inning —
ONE THOUSAND YEARS OF GLORY

LIFE HAS CERTAINLY changed for Manute Bol, a seven-foot, seven-inch tall Dinka from Turalei, Sudan. Manute now makes hundreds of thousands of dollars per year playing professional basketball in America. He came from a swampy, remote cattle town of mud and huts. Arab militias regularly burned villages, slaughtered livestock, and killed thousands of people in his home-land. Hundreds of thousands died from terrible famine. Manute survived a violent adolescence, some of which was dictated by tribal custom. Since leaving the Sudan in 1978, Bol has enjoyed a totally new life in the NBA. He is a premier shot-blocker. His life today bears little resemblance to his childhood existence.

When Jesus Christ returns to reign on earth for 1000 years, He will change the conditions of life even more than Manute Bol's circumstances have changed! The curse of sin will be lifted and all creatures will live in harmony, as the "law of the jungle" is repealed (Isaiah 11:1-9, 65:25). Ample rainfall is available over the re-newed earth (Isaiah 30:23) and land elevations around Jerusalem will be altered (Zechariah 14). Jesus Christ will rule as absolute dictator over all nations (Psalm 72) from Jerusalem (Isaiah 2:3) with righteousness, justice and faithfulness. His kingdom will continue forever (Psalm 89). Knowledge of the LordLordLord will cover the earth as waters cover the sea (Isaiah 11:9). Christ's subjects will live much longer (Isaiah 65:20) as they enjoy the peace, health, wealth, and prosperity He originally planned (Isaiah 2, 35, 62, 65; Psalm 72). Perfect justice will be the rule from the Perfect Judge (Isaiah 11:5, 32:16, 42:1-4, 65:21-23; Jeremiah 23, 31). Earth's population, which has been largely destroyed during the Great Tribulation, will soar (Jeremiah 30:20, 31:29; Ezekiel 47:22; Zechariah 10:8). The entire world will unite to worship Jesus (Zechariah 14:16-21). The temple is rebuilt in Jerusalem as a worship center. Animal sacrifices will again be offered as a reminder to an ideal world that the mighty Monarch, King Jesus Himself, once died to pay the penalty for sin (Jewish priests are now in training for such sacrifices!). Children born during this era must personally accept Jesus as Savior, just like anyone else in any other period of history. The sacrifices serve to remind them of the awfulness of sin. Only Jesus Christ can righteously change the world. The government is destined for His shoulders (Isaiah 9:6, 7). There will never be another time when Satan has authority as "prince and power of the air" or "god of this world" as he has today. Never again will man ruthlessly rule over his fellow man. What a change! What a King!

Read Revelation 20:7-10

And the devil, who deceived them, was thrown into the lake of
burning sulfur, where the beast and the false prophet had been
thrown. They will be tormented day and night forever and ever.

Revelation 20:10

Tenth inning —
SATAN'S LAST RALLY FALLS SHORT

THE 1962 WORLD SERIES between the Giants and the
Yankees came to a climatic end. San Francisco rallied in
the ninth inning of Game Seven in a desperate attempt
to win the game and the Series. With the bases loaded
and two outs, big Willie McCovey hit a scorching liner
that Yankee second baseman Bobby Richardson speared
for the final out. The Yankees had extinguished San
Francisco's last rally to win the Series in seven games!

Near the end of King Jesus' 1000 year reign on earth,
Satan will likewise mount one final futile rally. Verses 1-
3 of Revelation 20 tell us that Satan has been bound in
the Abyss during the Millennium. He is called by four
names in verse 2: dragon (for his cruelty); ancient serpent (for his continual guile and cunning treachery); the
devil (because he is an accuser, a deceiver, and a
tempter); and Satan (because he is our adversary).
Released for the final test of mankind, Satan again
roams the earth and gathers a great army from those
who have merely feigned obedience to the Wonderful
King, Jesus Christ. When they attack God's people in
the holy city, they are marching to their own deaths.
God destroys them all with a rain of fire from heaven.
The devil's rally is extinguished and he is thrown into a
lake of burning sulfur to be tormented forever!

What does Satan's final rally prove? Why should he
be allowed to tempt man one more time? His rally proves
that 1000 years of prison does not change his character.
He is never "rehabilitated" by his exile. It proves that
even ideal conditions will not make a person repent of

151

sin either, for a multitude of people born during the 1000 years of peace on earth still choose Satan over Jesus. "The heart is deceitful above all things and beyond cure. Who can understand it?" (Jeremiah 17:9). Only Jesus can change a person's life, but man must personally repent of sin. God has no grand-children. Finally, Satan's last rally proves again that God always judges evil. Though not in Hell today, Satan will spend eternity in a lake of burning sulfur. He is not a little gremlin in a red suit stoking hell's fire. He is not "Master of Hell." He suffers torment in a dark (Matthew 8:12), fiery place (Matthew 25:41). It is a place created just for him and his angels, but men who reject Jesus will suffer with him (Matthew 25:41). His last rally ends in total futility.

Read Revelation 21-22

Then I saw a new heaven and a new earth, for the first heaven and the first earth had passed away, and there was no longer any sea.

Revelation 21:1

Tenth inning —
ETERNITY: A WHOLE NEW BALL GAME

THOUGH THE GAME of baseball bears similarity to the original game as invented, in many respects it is entirely new and different. No one knows who first invented the game, but we do know it was played prior to 1839 and that it did not originate with Abner Doubleday in Cooperstown, NY. At one time, stakes were used for bases. In the 1840s, a runner could be "put out" by being hit with a thrown ball. Finally, in the spring of 1846, the New York Knickerbocker Club codified the rules. Still, there were no set number of innings. The game ended when a team scored 21 runs (then called "aces"). The pitcher stood only 45 feet from home plate, and the curve ball had not been invented yet!

Our lives on this earth resemble the rough beginnings of baseball. One day, when God makes all things new, we will look back and see that things today are as primitive as the origin of baseball. In eternity, we will have a new heaven and a new earth where there is no sin or temptation. We will live in the "New Jerusalem (a cube 1400 miles per side) where God and Jesus dwell! We will have radically different bodies and the law of gravity will be radically changed. No sun is needed, for Jesus provides all the light we need! There will be no night and we'll need no rest! We will eat fruit from the tree of life (Revelation 22:2). There is constant growth, development, and peace (Isaiah 9:6). It will be a "whole new ball-game" from the situations we know today!

Jesus said He was preparing a place for us (John 14:1-3). We will be with Him for eternity! God will ac-

153

complish His original purpose: fellowship with man who, as a free moral agent, has chosen to worship and serve Him eternally with no possibility of sin! We will be like Jesus (Romans 8:29), but will retain our own personalities for the glory of God! We will not live static lives, but will grow in grace and knowledge for all eternity.

What a prospect of joy and happiness awaits the believer in Jesus! All of heaven is free to those who come to Him by faith. The Spirit and the bride (church) say, "come!" And let him who hears say, "Come!" Whoever is thirsty, let him come; and whoever wishes, let him take the free gift of the water of life (Revelation 22:17). Are you thirsty? Come to Jesus today.

Appendices—
Scorecard
The Winning Run
The Perfect Reliever

ETERNITY John 1	1	2	3	4	5	6
	CREATION Genesis 1-2	FALL OF MAN Genesis 3	FLOOD Genesis 9	CALL OF ABRAHAM Genesis 12	THE NATION OF ISRAEL Exodus	ISRAEL STUMBLES Joshua Judges

Slaves in Egypt	Joshua enters the land
Delivered via Moses	Disobedience & defeat
The Law	King David
	Captivity & Return
	Artaxerxes' decree to rebuild Jerusalem Nehemiah 2
	7 weeks 49 years

Seventy week

SCORECARD
AND FUTURE (By Innings)

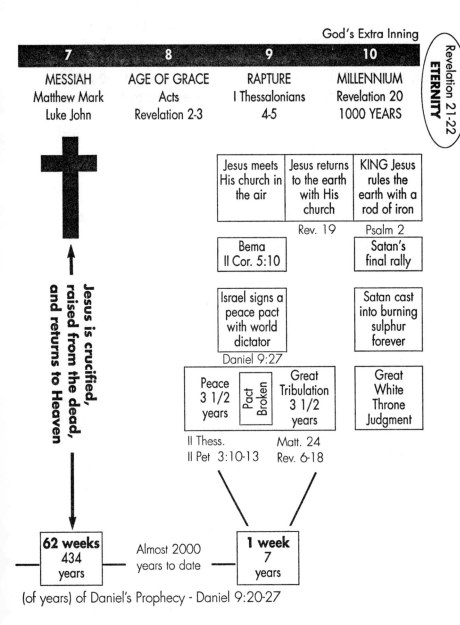

God's Extra Inning

7	8	9	10
MESSIAH	AGE OF GRACE	RAPTURE	MILLENNIUM
Matthew Mark	Acts	I Thessalonians	Revelation 20
Luke John	Revelation 2-3	4-5	1000 YEARS

Revelation 21-22
ETERNITY

Jesus is crucified, raised from the dead, and returns to Heaven

| Jesus meets His church in the air | Jesus returns to the earth with His church | KING Jesus rules the earth with a rod of iron |

Rev. 19   Psalm 2

| Bema II Cor. 5:10 | | Satan's final rally |

| Israel signs a peace pact with world dictator | | Satan cast into burning sulphur forever |

Daniel 9:27

| Peace 3 1/2 years | Pact Broken | Great Tribulation 3 1/2 years | Great White Throne Judgment |

II Thess.   Matt. 24
II Pet 3:10-13   Rev. 6-18

| **62 weeks** 434 years | Almost 2000 years to date | **1 week** 7 years |

(of years) of Daniel's Prophecy - Daniel 9:20-27

157

UNDERSTANDING THE SCORECARD

DANIEL WAS a godly young man who was carried into Babylonian (Iraqi) captivity when Jerusalem fell in 605 B.C. Daniel and his Jewish friends remained in exile for 70 years. During that time, God gave him some of the most far-reaching information ever revealed concerning the future. Gabriel's message to Daniel (Daniel 9:24-27) is a key to understanding what will happen to Israel and the world:

"Seventy sevens are decreed for your people and your holy city to finish transgression, to put an end to sin, to atone for wickedness, to bring in everlasting righteousness, to seal up vision and prophecy and to anoint the most holy.

"Know and understand this: From the issuing of the decree to restore and rebuild Jerusalem until the Anointed One, the ruler, comes, there will be seven 'sevens,' and sixty-two 'sevens.' It will be rebuilt with streets and a trench, but in times of trouble. After the sixty-two 'sevens,' the Anointed One will be cut off and will have nothing. The people of the ruler who will come will destroy the city and the sanctuary. The end will come like a flood: War will continue until the end, and desolations have been decreed. He will confirm a covenant with many for one 'seven.' In the middle of the 'seven' he will put an end to sacrifice and offering. And on a wing of the temple he will set up an abomination that causes desolation, until the end that is decreed is poured out on him.

Many Bible scholars understand the "seventy sevens" of Daniel's revelation to be seventy weeks of years, or 490 total years of God's direct dealing with Daniel's people, the Jews. God said He would accomplish six things in that time. The first three have to do with sin and the second three with the Kingdom of God."

1. "Finish Transgression" — God will finally stop Israel's tendancy to apostasy, to wander from Himself.
2. "Put an end to sin" — Sin will be removed, either by forgiveness for the repentent or by final judgment.
3. "To atone for wickedness" — Jesus was sent to die for Israel's sins (and for the sins of the world).
4. "To bring in everlasting righteousness" — Jesus will set up His kingdom on the earth and rule from Jerusalem.

5. "To seal up vision and prophecy" — Until fulfilled, prophecies are "unsealed." God will fulfill all He has said He would do during this time.
6. "To annoint the most Holy" — Jesus, the Holy One, will finally be enthroned where He belongs — on the throne of His father, David, in Jerusalem!

Daniel probably didn't understand everything he was told to write. Neither do we today! But let's examine what has happened and what could happen.

What Has Happened?

Gabriel said the "seventy sevens" would begin with the decree to rebuild Jerusalem. He gave Daniel this message in 539 B.C. In 444 B.C., the pagan King Artaxerxes issued the decree to rebuild Jerusalem (Nehemiah 2:1-8). It took 49 weeks (7 weeks of years), to rebuild the city. Four hundred and thirty-four years later (62 weeks of years), Jesus rode into Jerusalem on a donkey, was proclaimed King and promptly "cut off" (crucified) by His own people! So, the first two time periods ran consecutively and totaled 69 weeks (of years). There remains one more week (of years) of Daniel's prophecy for Israel!

It seems that God has postponed Israel's last week of years while He deals with His church — a mystery group not revealed until Jesus' rejection by the Jewish people. At that point, Jesus "had nothing" (v 26). His subjects rejected His kingdom and His kingship! So, Jesus offered the kingdom to "whosoever will" accept Him! Israel has suffered intensely since that day. In 70 A.D., the Roman general, Titus, leveled Jerusalem. As soldiers dismantled the temple seeking melted gold from the fires they set, not one stone was left upon another (Mark 13:1, 2; Luke 19:41-44)! Titus is said to have slaughtered five million Jews in one day! The Jewish people wandered around the world, homeless until 1948 when Israel dramatically became a nation once again.

What Will Happen Next?

The Jews are returning to their land today, but not with faith in their King Jesus.The stage is set for a false Messiah (John 5:43) who will gain their acceptance by promising them peace. This will happen just after the church is caught (raptured) away. When this pact is made, it will signal the beginning of Daniel's 70th week (of years). During this time, God totally fulfills His prophecies to Daniel and Israel. Though the Jews will think they have entered a wonderful new era (they will enjoy three and one-half years of peace), the false Messiah (antichrist) will break the agreement and three and one-half years of Great Tribulation for the Jews will begin. The events described in Revelation 6-18, Matthew 24, and Mark 13 make all previous persecutions of man and judgments of God seem minor by comparison.

Many scholars believe the rapture of the church and her appearance at the judgment seat ("bema") of Christ are the next events on God's calendar. If that is so, we must live faithfully for Him today. We have only a few years to prove faithful on earth, but all eternity to celebrate in Heaven!

Appendix II

The Winning Run

PERHAPS YOU HAVE READ this book, but never personally trusted the Savior with your earthly life and your
eternal destiny. The following baseball illustration explains
how you can come to know the Lord Jesus Christ:

In baseball, a runner must touch all four bases to score
a run for his team. The path to abundant and eternal life is
very similar to the base paths on a ball diamond.

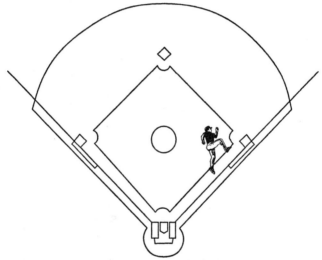

Step 1 (FIRST BASE) along that path is realizing that God
cares about you. He not only created you, but He also
loves you very deeply. He is seeking to give you an abundant life now and for eternity.

*For God so loved the world that He gave His one and only
Son, that whoever believes in Him shall not perish but
have eternal life.*

John 3:16

*I have come that they may have life, and have it to the
fullest.*

John 10:10

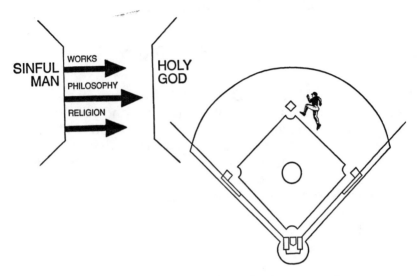

At SECOND BASE (step 2) we admit that we are sinners and separated from God. He is perfect, pure, and good; we are not. Because by nature we disobey Him and resist Him, He cannot have fellowship with us without denying His goodness and holiness. Instead, He must judge us.

Whoever believes in Him is not condemned; but whoever does not believe stands condemned already, because he has not believed in the name of God's one and only Son.
                                                            John 3:18

We realize we can never reach God through our own efforts. They do not solve the problem of our sin.

"or all have sinned and come short of the glory of God.
                                                            Romans 3:23

But your iniquities have separated you from your God; your sins have hidden His face from you, so that He will not hear.

                                                            Isaiah 59:2

For the wages of sin is death, but the gift of God is eternal life in Christ Jesus our Lord.

                                                            Romans 6:23

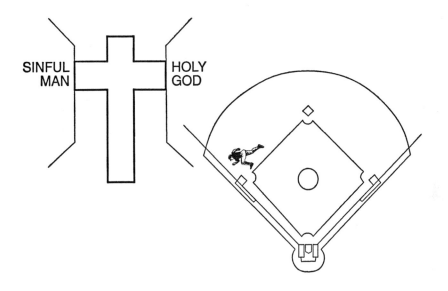

THIRD BASE is so close to scoring. Here (step 3) we understand that God has sent His Son, Jesus Christ, to die on the cross in payment for our sins. By His sacrifice, we may advance Home.

But God demonstrates His own love for us in this: While we were still sinners, Christ died for us.

Romans 5:8

For Christ died for sins once for all, the righteous for the unrighteous, to bring you to God.

I Peter 3:18

Jesus answered, "I am the way and the truth and the life. No one comes to the Father except through Me."

John 14:6

However, being CLOSE to Home does NOT count!

The Winning Run!

To score (step 4), we must personally receive Jesus Christ as Savior and Lord of our lives. We must not only realize that He died to rescue people from their sin but we must also trust Him to rescue us from our own sin. We cannot "squeeze" ourselves home any other way, and He will not force Himself upon us.

Yet to all who received Him, to those who believed in His name, He gave the right to become children of God.
John 1:12

For it is by grace you have been saved, through faith — and this is not from yourselves, it is the gift of God — not by works, so that no one can boast.
Ephesians 2:8-9

Why not receive Jesus Christ as your Savior and Lord right now? Simply say: "Yes, Lord," to His offer to forgive you for your sins and to change you.

_____
(signed)

_____
(date)

Tell someone of your decision and keep studying God's Word. These things greatly strengthen you (Romans 10:9-10). You may write *The Winning Run Foundation* for further encouragement. We would be thrilled to hear of your commitment! Welcome to eternal life!

THE WINNING RUN FOUNDATION
255B Settler's Road
Longview, TX 75605

Appendix III

The Perfect Reliever

THE FOLLOWING BASEBALL illustration explains how to walk consistently in the power of the Holy Spirit, our only hope for victory in spiritual warfare.

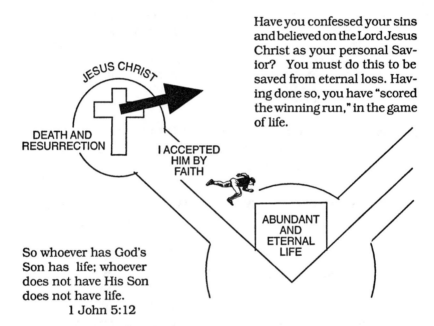

Have you confessed your sins and believed on the Lord Jesus Christ as your personal Savior? You must do this to be saved from eternal loss. Having done so, you have "scored the winning run," in the game of life.

So whoever has God's Son has life; whoever does not have His Son does not have life.
1 John 5:12

JESUS CHRIST

DEATH AND RESURRECTION

I ACCEPTED HIM BY FAITH

ABUNDANT AND ETERNAL LIFE

YOU SIGNED WITH THE WINNING TEAM WHEN YOU RECEIVED CHRIST!

1. Your sins were forgiven (Colossians 1:14).
2. You became a child of God (John 1:12).
3. God in dwelt you with His Spirit so you may live victoriously over the world (John 15:18-19), the flesh (Romans 7:15-18), and the devil (1 Peter 5:8).
4. You began the process of discovering God's purpose for your life (Romans 8:29).

BUT. . . .WHAT'S HAPPENING NOW?

165

Though our Lord has assured all His children of eternal life (John 10:28) and our position in Christ never changes, our practice may sometimes bring dishonor to God. The enemy rally makes life miserable.

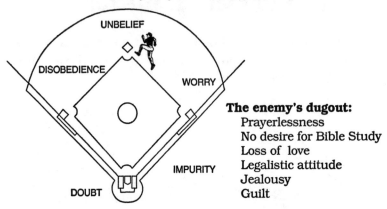

UNBELIEF

DISOBEDIENCE

WORRY

The enemy's dugout:
Prayerlessness
No desire for Bible Study
Loss of love
Legalistic attitude
Jealousy
Guilt

IMPURITY

DOUBT

This rally must be stopped, for the Bible makes it clear that no one who belongs to God can continually practice sin (I John 2:3; 3:6-10).

These two pitchers' mounds represent the two lifestyles from which a Christian must choose:

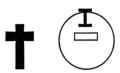

Self in control of the game and Christ's Resurrection power waiting in the bullpen — enemy rally produces discord.

Power of Christ replaces self on the mound — rally is stopped and peace is restored.

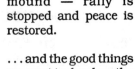

For we naturally love to do evil things that are just the opposite from the things that the Holy Spirit tells us to do;

... and the good things we want to do when the Spirit has His way with us are just the opposite of our natural desires.

Galatians 5:17a

SO, WHAT'S THE SOLUTION?

166

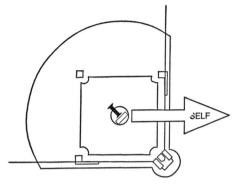

BRING IN THE PERFECT RELIEVER!

We must step off the mound and allow God to have complete authority by giving control of the game to the Holy Spirit.

Only by giving the Holy Spirit of God His rightful place of authority over our every thought, word and deed, can we consistently overcome defeat and despair.

If we are living now by the Holy Spirit's power, let us follow the Holy Spirit's leading in every part of our lives (Galatians 5:25).

WHAT DOES THE HOLY SPIRIT DO?

When you received Jesus Christ as Savior, the Holy Spirit *indwelt* you (Romans 8:9). Though all who have received Christ are indwelt by the Spirit, not all are *filled* (empowered, motivated) by the Spirit.

The Holy Spirit:
 a. Instructs us in all things (John 14:25-27).
 b. Always glorifies Jesus Christ (John 15:26; 16:13-15).
 c. Convicts us when things are wrong in our lives. (John 16:7-8).
 d. Helps us to share Christ with others (Acts 1:8).
 e. Assures us we belong to Christ (Romans 8:26).
 f. Enables us to live above circumstances through prayer (Romans 8:26).
 g. Flows from us as the source of an abundant and victorious life. (John 7:37-39).

HOW CAN YOU BE FILLED?

You can be filled (motivated) by the Holy Spirit right now IF YOU ARE WILLING to step off the mound of your life and give the ball to the Master Coach.

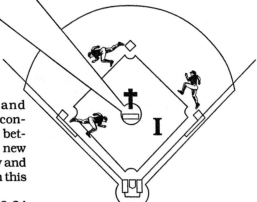

Now your attitudes and thoughts must all be constantly changing for the better. Yes, you must be a new and different person, holy and good. Clothe yourself with this new nature.

Ephesians 4:23-24

The Master Coach will not replace you on the mound against your heart's desire. Just as in receiving Christ, living consistently in His power is a matter of your will.

The Keys to Victory: Romans 6 (NAS)

A. KNOWING THIS, that our old self was crucified with Him that our body of sin might be done away with, that we should no longer be slaves to sin; for he who has died is freed from sin! (vs. 6-7)

B. Even so, CONSIDER YOURSELVES TO BE DEAD to sin, but alive to God in Christ Jesus. (v. 11)

C. But PRESENT YOURSELVES TO GOD as those alive from the dead, and your members as instruments of righteousness to God. (v. 13b)

PRESENT YOURSELF TO GOD THROUGH PRAYER

HERE IS A SUGGESTED PRAYER:

Dear Father,
I confess that I have taken control of my life and therefore have sinned against You. Thank You for forgiving me. I now CONSIDER myself dead to sin and PRESENT this body to You as a living sacrifice. I desire to be filled with Your Spirit as I live in obedience to Your WORD. Thank You for taking control of my life by the power of Your Spirit.

Amen.

HOW DO YOU KNOW YOU ARE FILLED BY THE HOLY SPIRIT?

 And we are sure of this, that He WILL listen to us whenever we ask Him for ANYTHING IN LINE WITH HIS WILL. And if we really KNOW He is listening when we talk to Him and make our requests, then we CAN BE SURE that He will answer us.　　　　　1 John 5:14-15

Is it God's will that you be filled (motivated) by His Spirit? He has said so (Ephesians 5:18). Therefore, based upon the authority of God's Word and His trust-worthiness, you can KNOW you are filled with His Spirit regardless of your emotions.

WHAT WILL GOD'S PERFECT RELIEVER ACCOMPLISH IN YOUR LIFE?

He will retire all doubt, fear, worry and other sins that run the bases of your life. He will substitute love, joy, peace and other fruits (Galatians 5:22-23). His assortment of pitches includes truth, faith, righteousness and other weapons through which daily victory is assured (Ephesians 6:10-18). He will turn your eyes to the Master Coach, Jesus Christ, and conform you to His likeness (II Corinthians 3:18). You can praise and thank God through trials and suffering in the game of life, knowing He has a plan for you (James 1:2-4). The final score will bring much glory to God!

WHAT IF SELF TRIES TO GET BACK INTO THE GAME?

The self life is a deadly enemy of the control of the Holy Spirit. Often self will try to return to the game, and when that happens, Satan quickly reloads the bases. If you sense this happening, take these steps:

1) Confess all known sin to God and thank Him. He has forgiven you (1 John 1:9).

2) Trust Christ to again fill you with the Holy Spirit, Who will once more take control (Ephesians 5:18).

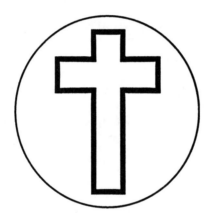

PLAYING THE GAME OF LIFE under His control will become a way of life, and you will experience constant victory! If "The Perfect Reliever" has been of help to you, please share it with a friend who also knows Jesus Christ as his personal Savior. He, too, can enjoy walking daily in the power of the Holy Spirit. May God bless you.

Elliot Johnson

For further information, please write:

WINNING RUN FOUNDATION
255B Settler's Road
Longview, TX 75605
170